The
Forgiveness
of
Sin

The
Forgiveness
of
Sin

by
TAD GUZIE
and
JOHN McILHON

THE THOMAS MORE PRESS
Chicago, Illinois

ISBN 0-88347-103-5

CONTENTS

PREFACE

Theologians usually reside in universities and often
have little to do with parish life. Pastors spend their
days ministering to every kind of need, from the
needs of people to broken water pipes, and often they
have little time left for reflection on their experience.
This book tries to bridge some of those gaps. It is a
collaborative effort between a pastor who took upon
himself the time-consuming discipline of writing
about his experiences, and a theologian who left university life to work for a local church.

Tad Guzie is responsible for chapters 3, 5, 6, and
9. These chapters re-use materials that originally appeared in *What A Modern Catholic Believes about
Confession* (Thomas More Press, 1975), which has
been out of print for some time. The materials have
been revised in the light of the Catholic Church's new
rite of penance. John McIlhon is responsible for
chapters 2, 8, and 10. Both of us had a hand in
chapters 1, 4, and 7. The latter chapter contains
materials that appeared in the *U.S. Catholic* ("Why

PREFACE

They Changed Confession," September 1976).

The *experience* of sin and forgiveness is one thing.
How we *ritualize* that experience, or how we celebrate it sacramentally, is another. The first four chapters center around the experience of sin and reconciliation. Chapters 5 and 6 look at the ways in which
Christians have ritualized this experience, from New
Testament times up to our own. The final four chapters take up many dimensions of the Church's new
penance rites. Throughout the book, we look at the
experiences of Catholics today, the pains of transition
from old to new, and many challenges for the future.

Chapter 1

THE ELDER SON AND THE GETTING OF GRACE

Confession has been a mixed experience for me. Sometimes it has been a real release from the burden of sin. At other times it has been simply a burden. And sometimes it has been a nonexperience: What in the world am I doing here?

It would seem that a definite majority of otherwise practicing Catholics have given up confession as any sort of regular religious practice. For many, it is only the leftover of an old religious habit which brings them to the confessional a couple of times a year. And when they get there, they wonder just what they are doing there. No use invoking the old idea of confession as a means of increasing God's grace in one's soul. Many Catholics have long since moved away from the idea of grace as some kind of divine quantity that is going to be increased through the correct performance of a ritual. If the ritual of confession has been consistently distasteful, as it has for many people, how can it really be an occasion of grace for them?

The Church has now given us a new rite of penance. By this time most Catholics have become familiar with the external features of the rite for individual confession: a confessional room instead of the dark box; the option of face-to-face confession without a screen; scripture readings and new prayers. Some people have experienced another form of sacramental penance: a communal celebration with general absolution.

But there are no signs that hordes of people are returning to the practice of frequent confession. As for communal celebrations, many pastors fear that people seek general absolution as a means of avoiding the burden of confessing privately to a priest. Later on we will take up the different forms of sacramental penance and talk about them in detail. For the moment, I simply want to point out that the revision of a rite is much more than a matter of moving furniture, rewriting prayers, or replacing individual absolution with general absolution. As the past decade has taught us, a truly renewed liturgy calls for renewed attitudes, even entirely *new* attitudes, on the part of all the faithful and their ministers.

Before we take up these new attitudes, let us look at a few of the old ones. There are three attitudes in particular which get in the way of our understanding the new rite of penance.

The first can be called the *syndrome of the elder son.* Everyone knows the parable of the Prodigal Father, but few of us find it easy really to believe in it. The father had never stopped loving his son, and he welcomed him instantly. He wasn't even interested in hearing the boy's confession. Just bring on the fatted calf, and let's rejoice at his return!

But this is not the way human justice works, and it is not the way we have generally viewed the sacrament of penance. The practice of this sacrament has been dominated by the attitude of the elder son: Hold the fatted calf! Let's get a few things cleared up first. Make your speech, recite your list of sins, give some guarantees, and prove yourself worthy to join the rest of us who haven't strayed.

This attitude was fostered by the legalism which gradually crept into the practice of confession. One major challenge of the new rite is whether we can overcome this legalism and the syndrome of the elder son.

A second attitude that affects our understanding of sacramental penance can be called the *problem of religionized sin.* Abraham Maslow makes the point that where one area of experience is religionized, the rest of life can easily be secularized. "The experiences of the holy, the sacred, the divine, of awe, of creatureliness, of surrender, of mystery, of piety, thanksgiving, gratitude, self-dedication, if they happen at all, tend to be confined to a single day of the week, to happen under one roof of one kind of structure only, under certain triggering circumstances only, to rest heavily on the presence of certain traditional, powerful, but intrinsically irrelevant, stimuli, e.g. organ music, incense, chanting of a particular kind, certain regalia, and other arbitrary triggers." The result of such religionizing is that people are often "absolved from the necessity or desire to feel these experiences at any other time."[1]

One of the most obvious examples of this phenomenon is the idea of going to church in order to find God. According to the Gospel, this is to put the matter the wrong way around, the old case of the cart before the horse. In the Christian view of things a church is a gathering place for people who come there to worship together precisely because they find God and the things of God in their ordinary lives.

Attitudes toward sin can also be affected by the phenomenon described by Maslow. For many Catholics, the experience of sin was "religionized" by the traditional catalogues of mortal and venial sin. Those catalogues got repeated use in the recital of sins in the confessional. Maybe we always knew the limitations of those categories. Maybe we even knew our own real sinfulness. But what was one supposed to *say* in the confessional?

For some, one of the results of dropping the practice of frequent confession has been to let awareness of failure and inadequacy and a lot of things that used to be called plain and simply "sin" fall outside the realm of religion and the sacraments.

It is one thing to come to the realization that "mortal sin" is not a frequent event in the life of the ordinary person who is trying to live like a Christian. The pity of the old catechism is that it presented sin as an idea rather than a reality, a concept rather than an experience.

Still, for all of this, it is quite another thing to think

that we are not sinful people, or that there is no such thing as genuine "sin." One can easily grant the fact that few committed Christians fulfill the Baltimore Catechism's requirements for full-blown mortal sin: grave matter, full knowledge and full consent. But the alternative to being in that state of mortal sin was being "in the state of grace." And it is hard to see how mature Christians can dare to think they are in that traditional "state of grace" in a world where we have been made aware that a perfectly normal and accepted American search for comfort and enjoyment of the good life involves exploitation of someone, some individual, some group, be it only those distant and unknown persons who pick vegetables for our tables.

So for many Catholics, the consciousness of real honest-to-goodness sinfulness no longer has much to do with the "sacrament of penance." The old form of the sacrament never really trained people to deal with anything but specific and nameable offenses, almost in a courtroom style. The interested and committed Christian has now developed a type of social and moral awareness that defies the old categories of mortal and venial sins, nameable and numberable in a "good confession."

What many Catholics today experience as true sinfulness just can't be related to the confessional. Or let's put it the other way around: Everyday contribution to and participation in the sinful structures of life is, for many Catholics, not something that belongs to the forum of confession. Confession is only for "religionized sin." New types of Christian awareness, which have to do more with sinful*ness* than with explicit *sins,* fall outside the realm of sacramental penance.

It is often difficult for people to pin down their reasons for feeling culpable about some situations in which they find themselves, or to articulate *why* we feel that somehow we have failed to deal with a situation in a Christian manner. But, as we were all taught, the minimum requisite for a "good confession" consists in reciting what kind of sins we committed and the number of times we committed them. The result of this religionizing of sin, for many, has been that the ritual has little relation to those situations in which sin is in fact most deeply and personally *experienced.*

A third attitude that affects our understanding of penance is the whole matter of coming to the sacraments to *get grace.*

When I was a child, milk was my image of grace. I have the Baltimore Catechism to thank for that. How vividly I remember the picture of two milk bottles illustrating sin and grace. The "sin" bottle was empty and the "grace" bottle full. If you sin, I was taught, your soul will always be empty of God's grace. If, however, you pray, receive the sacraments often, and be a good boy, you will get more and more grace. Only full bottles get to heaven because Christianity is the milky way—at least that's how it came across to me.

Not long after that, a theological problem began to develop in my nine-year-old head. I was taught that there were two kinds of grace, sanctifying and actual.

Milk was milk to me and how come, I thought, God gives us two kinds of "milk"?

One morning I solved the problem. It happened when I brought our daily delivery of milk from the porch. Since milk was not homogenized in those days, I carried the bottle in the same careful way one carries nitroglycerin—mixing cream and milk, be it noted, was an explosive issue with my mother. As I carefully set the bottle of milk down, I suddenly saw the solution to my theological problem. The rich cream standing gloriously atop the lowly skimmed milk—aha! Why hadn't I noticed this before? Sanctifying grace was like cream because that's what really counts for heaven, and actual grace was like skimmed milk because it was just the ordinary day-to-day stuff needed for ordinary daily living.

Later that day, I shared my theological insight with the teacher who in turn used it to further reinforce the grand and glorious theological-milkshake perspective of grace that was evolving in our religion class.

As a teenager, my milky-way understanding of grace began to vanish and I didn't know what grace was or meant. So I settled on some kind of vague idea that grace was a thing God gives if we pray, fast, receive sacraments, and obey commandments. If you do "them" you'll get "it." Not quite as neat as milk, but I was nourished.

Then came a fateful day. While reading the daily paper I came across the report of a speech delivered by Monsignor Luigi Ligutti, then secretary of the National Rural Life Conference in Des Moines. Monsignor Ligutti described parishes as "sacramental filling stations" where millions of Catholics were going each Sunday to be filled with divine fuel to keep them going for another week.

My system was under attack again! Why was I going to Mass and confession if there was nothing to get? Why did I pray and fast if these spiritual works didn't procure something? Why bother with the ten commandments if their strict observance is nothing more than an ethical code? My neat and tidy system of grace was crumbling.

At any rate, I decided to hang in there and continue my search.

The seminary didn't help. Grace was neither milk nor gasoline. It was "gift," "habit," "quality," "created," "uncreated," "antecedent," "consequent," and of course, "sanctifying and actual." Despite all these new labels one thing was for sure—you still had to *get* it.

My first real break came not in the classroom but in reading the poem of Gerard Manley Hopkins, "God's Grandeur." The poem provided me with a new understanding of God's grace and it has remained with me to this day.

The world is charged with the grandeur of God.
    It will flame out, like shining from shook foil;
    It gathers to a greatness, like the ooze of oil
Crushed. Why do men then now not reck his rod?
Generations have trod, have trod, have trod;
    And all is seared with trade; bleared, smeared with toil;

And wears man's smudge and shares man's smell:
the soil is bare now, nor can foot feel, being shod.

And for all this, nature is never spent;
    There lives the dearest freshness deep down things;
And though the last lights off the black West went
    Oh, morning, at the brown brink eastward, springs
    —Because the Holy Ghost over the bent
World broods with warm breast and with ah!
bright wings.[2]

As I reflected on this poem, it became clear to me
that the God I was trying to "get" had already graced
this world with his presence. His son Jesus Christ
came to "get" me, and to favor me with his love. He
did not hesitate to wear my "smudge" and share my
"smell". Like Francis Thompson's "Hound of
Heaven" he had always pursued me as I trod to find
God who had already graced me with his grandeur.
Bleared, seared, and smeared by empty and useless
toil, I finally stopped long enough to be warmed by
his breast and enfolded by his bright wings.

As far as God is concerned, grace is his loving
presence in this spirit-filled world. As far as we are
concerned, grace is the growing awareness, consciousness and actualizing of his presence in our history. Once we experience God's love, once we let it
"flame out like shining from shook foil," we can
know the meaning of grace. There's really nothing to
get because God's love has already begotten us.

"Getting grace," then, is not the issue. The real
issue is a renewal of attitudes which shape our under-

standing of God, Church, sacraments, sin, and grace. When I perceived God as the one out there I was searching to get, this led me to perceive my faith as a number of things to do to "get" God. This understanding of God and his loving presence, "thingy" as it was, robbed me of a priceless perception that he is our Father and we are his children. We are related to God, not things. Once I understood that grace is the deepening of a relationship with God and with others, my understanding of church and sacraments took on an entirely new meaning.

What a relief to discover that the Church is not a sacramental filling station with seven heavenly hoses pumping graced gas from a God up there into souls down here. Rather, the Church is a graced, loved people in union with the God who is with them. He is Emmanuel. The Church is a graced and loved people united with one another in a community whose christened light "flames out like shining from shook foil" attracting, calling, inviting, yes even hounding humankind to life in Christ.

When our understanding of grace shifts, everything else shifts. From what I have said concerning grace, you can see that the shift is from quantities of grace to the quality of our acceptance, appreciation, awareness, and consciousness of God's loving presence and his relationship with us. What did the prodigal son "get" when he returned to his father? He "got" a new appreciation, awareness, and consciousness of what he had already had before he left his father's home. The festive clothes, ring, fatted calf, and sumptuous banquet, not to speak of the father's affection and love were already a part of the son's life before the young man decided to kick up his heels to search for the goodies he foolishly imagined he didn't have. And when he discovered in a pigpen that life in his father's servants quarters was a good deal more plush, he "got" quite an awakening.

The new rites of the Church have turned out to be an occasion for just such an awakening.

Chapter 2

THE EXPERIENCE OF CHURCH

"Bertha's Motel" is what a lot of people lovingly call my aunt Bertha's home in a small central Iowa town. Her home is like a motel because you can find people there all the time. They feel at home because they feel welcome.

I go to "Bertha's Motel" frequently. I know every inch of the house as if it were my own home. One afternoon I dropped in to see her. After nearly an hour, Bertha said, "My goodness, haven't you noticed something different in this room?" I looked around. Everything looked the same—the sofa, coffee table, familiar pictures on the walls, plants tastefully arranged around the room, and the cuckoo clock at the foot of the stairway vying for attention every half hour.

I frowned.

"Keep on looking," she coaxed with a goading laugh.

Suddenly I saw what was different. A painting of Bertha's childhood home in Vermont had been replaced by a shelf displaying a beautiful antique clock. The clock, she told me, presided for over 100 years in the kitchen of her family home. Why I failed to notice the clock for almost an hour I don't know. It is far more conspicuous than the painting it replaced and, in fact, is the focal point of the room.

When I walked into the living room of my aunt's home that day, the clock was already there. As far as I was concerned, however, it was not there to me. I was not conscious of its presence. On the other hand, the clock was not made absent just because I wasn't conscious of its presence. I didn't bring the clock into the room when I became conscious of it. I didn't "get" the clock from my aunt. What I "got" was a consciousness of its presence through the consciousness-raising process of Bertha's prodding.

The story of the clock is how I understand the meaning of grace in relationship to the sacraments. Baptism, for example, initiates persons into the graced relationships of families and communities whose own deep and ever-growing consciousness of God's presence leads the newly initiated into the consciousness of love in those relationships.

As a pastor, my attitude toward baptism has changed because my perspective has changed. My first concern is the parents. Are they conscious of God's decisive presence in all of the relational experiences their children will absorb? Are the parents persuaded that baptism calls them to provide an all-pervading faith atmosphere wherein the children will gradually be able to perceive the mystery of their own graced lives as they become conscious of God's loving presence in that graced atmosphere?

A priest can pour buckets of water on a baby. But if that child grows up in a dog-eat-dog atmosphere of hostility, dissension, greed, selfishness, and indifference to religious values, baptism will mean little. Baptism for children living in such an atmosphere is not saving because their graceless atmosphere is not saving.

This does not necessarily mean doing away with infant baptism. But let's do away with the schizophrenic attitude that the priests, sisters, and lay catechists take care of the children's religious values, while mom and dad run day-care centers after the kids get home from school. This madness isn't working and it never has.

Similarly, does a person become a Catholic merely because he or she spent three or four months listening to a priest doggedly wending his way through a catechism? Is that the criterion for baptism? Is this kind of initiation adequate to sustain the newly baptized for a lifetime commitment to a community he or she has hardly been introduced to? Can the Spirit of Christ and his Church be taught as catechumens are taught in the less than inspiring atmosphere of the pastor's phone-ringing office? And when the last drop of water rolls off the forehead of the newly initiated, is that all there is? Are the newly baptized merely introduced to a font, or are they initiated into a loving community of friends whose holiness attracted them in the first place, who have had a significant role in their Christian formation, and who now welcome them to share in the community's own consciousness of God's covenanted love?

Baptism is pivotal for understanding the sacraments and the love of God they celebrate. All of the sacraments initiate us into new dimensions of Christian consciousness. A couple is wedded at the altar. Their marriage is a life-long deepening of a graced relationship covenanted at that altar. Each day holds for them the opportunity to deepen their relationship and to experience new dimensions of God's love as they live the graced process of becoming one. Is not their marriage a constant renewal of their baptismal commitment to the plan and the vision of Jesus, "Father may they be one as you are in me and I am in you"?

And what of the eucharist? Is our Sunday obligation one of mere physical presence in order to "get" God's attention? Does our physical presence alone win from God assurance of instant divine favor? Is Sunday Mass nothing more than the weekly fulfillment of a contract whereby God gives grace to individuals in exchange for an hour of their time? Or is the Sunday eucharist a community celebration of both God's real and realized presence as that community labors to become one in Jesus the Lord? Is the Sunday eucharist a joyful witness of a community whose daily experiences of God's presence causes them to acknowledge with power and conviction that Jesus is really present in our lives? Is Sunday worship a true testimony of the ongoing process of oneness and wholeness we call reconciliation?

Today's youth may be the ones who will lead us to

a new appreciation of grace, paradoxical as that appears. For example, young people cannot buy into the obligation mentality which requires mere physical presence at Sunday mass. They crave a lot more involvement. They are not objecting to the eucharist. They object to a "thingy" mentality which separates eucharist (rite) from life. They are reluctant to ritualize when the ritual does not appear to flow out of their experience of life. If the eucharist is merely the "thing" they do on Sunday, interrupting the other things going on in their lives, they cannot accept the fact that their Church obligates them to that. For them, eucharist is a verb as well as a noun.

I enjoy listening to young people as they express their thoughts about God, Church, sacraments, grace and salvation. Let me share some of their thoughts from what they write and say.

From a seventeen-year-old American exchange student in Holland: "You really grasp what is meant by Church and community. Here I am thousands of miles from home, sitting in a church not unlike many in the States praying and singing in a different language and realizing—hey!—these people are of a whole different culture than mine. Yet they gather here in this church, same as me, with a wish to give of themselves, their time, and their thoughts, to the Lord. You know, that gives me a feeling of never really being lonely. I shall always keep in mind that probably the most rewarding Sundays were when I couldn't understand a single word that was being said. You can still apply the old cliche—you only get out of the mass what you put into it. Once you do put in, you'll be able to put out—you'll be able to share someone with others."

A "rap" session with high school juniors: "I am freer to think today. That's a good thing, but there's a problem with this. When I was little, I thought of God as a nice old man. So did my parents. Everyone's idea of God was the same. But then came the sixties, you know, the 'God is dead' stuff. Pow! You go like instant tea all the way from the nice old man to—well-maybe there is no God. I've got to decide. I'm caught in the middle. What do I do with my freedom?"

"I have the impression that years ago people's childhood ideas of God lasted them a lifetime. I think that's what's wrong with a lot of adults today. It's impossible to let your seven-year-old God be your fifty-year-old God. Either you choose who God is here and now as you grow, or you drop out. Why do a lot of kids drop out? Because their parents want them to worship *their* seven-year-old image of God while we suspect that God is either a lot more than that or he isn't at all.

"I think we learn at school more about the human make-up than our parents did. One of my teachers has been explaining to us the levels of maturity. Very interesting! Many people never leave a lower level of maturity because the lower the level, the more secure and comfortable you feel. The higher you go, the more opportunity for choice and decision. That's threatening to the immature mind because decision-making isn't all that safe and sure-fire.

"Maybe that's why there is such a hassle in parish life. It goes back to your image of God. If God is the 'nice old man' who will take care of everything in exchange for an hour a week, a confession once in a while, a couple of bucks a week for good measure, and a few Hail Marys before you go to bed at night, then your back is going to get up when the pastor talks about community, shared responsibility, and justice. It's kind of scary when you find out that maybe the 'nice old man' isn't going to do everything —you know, presto! I think God challenges me to deliver a whole lot more of myself than one hour a week."

"When you stop to think about it, community is a challenge. It's hard to give yourself to others— that's scary too. It's also scary to think that others have something to give to you. The ego takes a beating there. It's much easier to have a God out there who pats my head down here. Lots of times I wish for a perfect God who doesn't challenge me to his perfection. Really, that's what community amounts to. It challenges us to the kind of unity God is in the first place. God is community and it takes a high level of maturity even to be aware of that, let alone do it.

"Religion has got to include everything human or it just isn't religion. I really don't think kids are turning off religion. I think they turn off what passes for religion."

"That's true, but kids are also like some adults at a low level of maturity. Let's not kid ourselves, a lot of us see the implications of community. You've got to give yourself—produce! That's work. Every once in a while I catch myself wanting a Latin mass. I'll admit it. I remember the Latin mass when I was a little kid. Father did it all, just like Father ran the parish. It was all pretty secure, safe, a nice warm feeling. But I also tell myself that if that's all I want in religion, am I true to myself, to God, and the Church?"

"There's another way of being caught in the middle. Some kids don't want to pay the price of building the Church. That's a bit much for them. At the same time, they don't want the 'nice old man' image of God either because maybe their parents have that image. They've decided against both and just drop out."

"When you talk about community, you're not talking about any old kind of community. We could go about creating community without God. Sometimes I think we are doing that in the Church especially in religious education. I'd like to see us get back to beginnings—roots. Like, what is faith? Do doubts have value? Why is Jesus the Messiah? For that matter, why is God important? Why believe in God? What difference does God make in my life? What's the connection between God and Church? Just what does salvation mean? A lot of kids I know don't even believe in God. Yet, they say they believe in loving one another. They'll talk community too, but God isn't in it. When we get to that point, do we have a community or a club that does goodies for others? I guess what I'm saying is, we had better get back to the root beliefs of religion, like what basic difference does God make in community? I don't want a return to the Baltimore Catechism rigidity. But I feel that in our effort to throw out rigidity, we may have thrown out some fundamentals."

"When you say fundamentals, that reminds me of fundamentalists. This 'born again' stuff has made me think, I'll admit. But there's something wrong with this. It's too slick, too easy, not real. It's hard for me to believe that what's so common and necessary in dealing with others is not necessary, apparently, in our relationships with God. I mean this. I have to renew my relationships with others if I want to keep and deepen my relationships with them. Isn't this true with God? This once-and-for-all business bothers me. 'Born again' is okay if you understand it right. I think every time you're introduced to a new image of God, you're 'born again.' There is a lot of God I don't know and haven't experienced. That's why I'd like to know more about the Jews, Buddha, the Hindus, and the Moslems. They've been around a lot longer than Christianity. I often wonder, is Christianity a kind of composite of all these images of God? Are the truths of these religions completely false? I don't think so. I feel that if I can understand their truths, I can understand the teachings of Jesus better. If for example, I can really understand what the Jews meant by messiah, why Jesus didn't fit their 'job description,' then maybe when I read the gospel I can see for myself why Jesus claimed to be the messiah. If I can see that, I'm 'born again,' at least a little more than I am now."

"Speaking of 'born again': there's another way of looking at this. I've been thinking lately that maybe the sacraments like eucharist and reconciliation are ways to be 'born again.' Sometimes young people leave the Church too quickly without really going into what the Church teaches. They hear all about being born again and figure, 'well, I haven't had that experience so I'll join a 'born again' religion so I can get something the Catholic Church hasn't given me.' They seem to want instant religion along with everything else that's instant today. Quite frankly, I enjoy the Mass. I think the reason is that I lectored ever since I was in grade school, have made banners, and helped plan our youth liturgies. I know now that if I want a better liturgy in our parish, I have to share my talents. That means that the Mass challenges me to grow. I feel sure now that because of this, I have a new image of God. I feel like I'm sharing in his work.

"Then I think, hey, if the world is to be better I have to make it better. So, in a real way, the Mass has made me more conscious of my relationship with God and with the world. I've heard my teachers say, 'The Mass is a sign of life.' I think I understand that now. For me anyway, the Mass is one sacrament which has caused me to be 'born again.' I mean a new image of God has been born in me."

"I guess what I have to say about the Church is along the lines of pet peeves. I've noticed that people are so picky. Some people don't like the pastor, so they close their pocketbooks. There's a lot of that today. Other picky people bug out of their parish and gallop over to a parish where things are more to their liking. Picky people are too concerned with things. I'm tired of things. Personally, I'm trying to sort out in my mind the really basic changes in my daily life called for by the changes in the liturgy. Take communion in the hand. I know people who let that throw them into a tizzy. But that's only a minor change and all it's saying is, 'Look, you've got Jesus in your hand, what do you do with him today?' I work with my hands. Receiving the eucharist in my hands is simply saying, 'If the kingdom is ever to come to you, you have to work with me.' That's beautiful!

"Along with that, there's got to be more to confession than a routine reciting of sins. Sin is deep inside you. It's got something to do with not being who you really are. Confession changed with me when I began to learn in school about relationships. I began to think, 'so that's why sin is so bad—it destroys relationships.' I'm not interested merely in telling sins. I'm interested in the commitment to Christ's life my confessions are making me more conscious of. How I treat others, how I relate to them, is how I am discovering the meaning of Jesus."

"Me too. I want a direction to go. I think the new way of confession does that much better than the old. What good are five Our Fathers and five Hail Marys?

That's anti-climactic. The old rite was unfitting. Do you mean to tell me that five and five does it? The whole thing was kind of deceptive.

"The new way of going to confession kind of says, 'Keep dealing with your wounds.' It gives me a way to deal with them. A priest told me one time that conversion is always going on. The old rite did not give me that impression. You said your five and five, and bang! It was supposed to be done. Well, I knew in my heart it wasn't. Now I see why regular confession is necessary. My life in Christ has to be renewed —just like friendships."

"Priests are more helpful now. They are human and you can see that when you go face to face. The priest is part of the sacrament and I'm part of the sacrament. I used to think of the sacrament of penance as a computer—you know, put in the information and out comes the reformation."

"One thing I would like to see. The new rite could be more prayerful. I like it when the priest prays for me and asks me to pray too. I really feel the closeness of God and that he loves me because I'm special. I wish more priests would do that. Maybe they will . . ."

And so it went for two and a half hours. In fact, one of the teenagers said, "Hey Father, let's do this again!" Young people have not turned off the "dearest freshness deep down things." They resonate to the freshness because like all youth they themselves are fresh. They spot the freshness and want to run with it.

If I were to identify one word that characterized this two-and-a-half-hour session it is *care*. These young people care for the Church and want it to be all that it can be. They want others to care also. They appreciate the listening of others because they definitely have something to say. They too listen when the speaker exhibits the care they hunger for. They seem to be saying, "If you care you've got the cure."

I rejoice that today the Church is rediscovering her roots. For if the Church, with mounting urgency, proclaims her ancient legacy of message, community, and service, and witnesses to that legacy, the youth will be back to celebrate because that legacy is where their intuition and instincts lie. They hunger for truth, for loving relationships, and for the opportunity to do justice.

Today's Church is beginning to resonate to this hunger. The Church has something to offer to satisfy the hungers of both young and old. And when our youth hear what's afoot in the Church, in the "dearest freshness deep down things," they will come back to the Church eucharistic-bound, and with joyful enthusiasm bring back those of us who are under the illusion that we never left.

Chapter 3

THE EXPERIENCE OF SIN

Every Catholic is familiar with the catechism's distinction between "mortal" and "venial" sin. These categories attempt to objectify various extremes of behavior, the two ends of the spectrum of sinfulness. They say nothing about the Christian's progress through inadequacy and failure toward the full freedom of the children of God—or if I may amend Paul's phrase, the full freedom of adults of God.

A morally mature Christian can understand what the mortal-venial distinction is trying to get at. The difficulty is that the distinction does not create morally mature Christians, and it can often be counterproductive as a catechetical device. If one operates only out of these categories, the result is often an introverted, self-centered morality which finally leads to travesties like the classic question "How far can I go before it's a mortal sin?" The *Christian* question is rather "What should I be?" A true answer to that question, and the starting point for a Christian conscience and a Christian theology of sin and forgiveness, is the awareness and frank confession that I am not what I should be, and I frequently fail to work at what I should be.

But such an awareness does not develop overnight, either in the history of humankind's religious experience or in our own personal histories. Sin is an experience, not a concept. And our concepts of what "sin" is undergo change, as we undergo a normal process of human growth.

In the gospel of John, at the beginning of the story of the man born blind, the disciples ask Jesus, "Rabbi, was it his sin or that of his parents that caused him to be born blind?" (Jn 9:2). This is where our human consciousness of sin begins: sin is seen as a disruption of some cosmic order, violation of a system. The violation brings about a physical punishment which would not have occurred if the system had not been tampered with.

At this stage of consciousness, as Ricoeur suggests, sin is experienced as *defilement.* Jesus' friends think of the man born blind as a victim of defilement, as one whose physical defect is somehow a result of moral failure on someone's part. For at a primitive stage of religious awareness, the *ethical* order is not differentiated from the *physical* order. "Doing ill" is not distinguished from "faring ill." Physical events like disease, sickness and death are not clearly distinguished from moral events, from the human actions which generate ethical and social evils like injustice and war and exploitation. Nor is God distinguished from nature, or from the system of cause and effect that operates in the natural world. This means that if I am suffering something, it must be a punishment sent by God, a punishment for some violation of the system.

Our earliest codes of behavior have to do with keeping the human community in harmony with the outer world, and thus protecting the supply of food. Violation of a taboo is an extremely serious matter because it threatens the food supply; such a violation might cause the guardian spirits to withdraw from the processes of nature or to unleash punishment and death upon the tribe. Motive does not matter.

In a modern society, the law makes distinctions according to degrees of willful intent—murder in the first degree, manslaughter, etc. Such distinctions do not exist at the dawn of human consciousness. Motives do not matter because people are not yet conscious of them; human persons have not yet awakened to their freedom, their interior autonomy and distinctness from the fixed processes of nature. If a taboo is violated, the gravity of the violation is determined strictly by *what* was done, not *why* it was done.

We can watch children go through this same process of emerging consciousness. For a small child, accidentally dropping and breaking a whole stack of dinner plates is a "worse sin" than throwing down a single plate in anger. We do good and bad things long before we are able to reflect on the meaning of good and bad. At first, all we know is what brings approval from mommy and daddy, and what brings a spanking. Children are naturally preoccupied with establishing a workable relationship with the whole system surrounding them.

This workability is at first unmoral, or not yet moral. The rules of the game of life have to be learned first, and children's attitudes toward that game are accurately reflected by the other games they play: they argue about exact rules and they enforce the rules strictly, down to the last detail. "Why these rules?" is a much later question than "What are the rules?" It is pointless to ask *why* one mustn't step on the cracks in the sidewalk; all that matters is that you break the rules of the game if you do. In short, children try to set up a stable relationship with the forces surrounding them long before they begin to discover that they possess a freedom in the face of those forces, that they can actually ask whether a rule is useful or practical or just.

Whatever we tell children about a loving God takes hold only gradually. A child's early experiences of the outside world center around satisfaction and rejection, reward and punishment. And so, for all of us as for primitive races, the notion of an *enforcing* God is much more basic and psychically more natural than that of a *loving* God. Primitives feared their deities because those deities were identified with the fearsome life-giving and death-dealing forces of nature. Children will tend to have the same fear, even if they are never taught such fear, because for a long time God is indistinct from parents and authorities and all the other systems that surround them. Clearly, if children experience genuine love from their parents, the groundwork is laid for their understanding of a loving God. But that God will have to compete with the God-concept that very naturally emerges from children's other experiences of authorities and systems.

There is a long way to go before the father-God becomes more than a paternalistic God. This is true in the history of our religious tradition, and it is true for each of us personally. The loving father who unhesitatingly welcomes the prodigal son simply because he loves him is many years of psychic and religious growth removed from the warrior-god who visits plagues on the naughty pharaoh. Insofar as God is undifferentiated from other systems, he is bound to be conceived as the ultimate enforcer of the rules and therefore the authority most to be feared.

The *Reader's Digest* and the Sunday supplements invariably contain articles telling us about how we are to grow up, shuck off the infantile, become adults. But there is at least one area where society permits us to indulge in the infantile, and that area, unfortunately, is religion. Religion is all too easily used as an enforcement or justification for primitive attitudes and God-concepts which adult society quite rightly does not accept. Insofar as we maintain an infantile attitude toward other *persons,* we react to them strictly as forces which bring us satisfaction or as forces which bring disapproval or rejection. It takes a lot of growing to realize that other people cannot be dealt with in this way. If I am to become an adult, I have to realize that other people are not objects to be used; they are subjects like myself, they have a value beyond *my* satisfaction.

In a similar way, insofar as one retains an infantile attitude toward *God,* the final and most meaningful thing to be said about him is that he rewards me if I am good and punishes me if I am bad. If there is any insight that typifies our Judeo-Christian understanding of the deity, it is that God is *personal*—not an object or being to be used in a sub-personal manner (as we unfortunately tend to use other persons at an immature stage of relationship), but one to be dealt with at the center of one's personhood. At an infantile stage of consciousness, however, God is not dealt with seriously as subject, as personal, as other. God has no value, no meaning beyond *my* satisfaction; and as a matter of fact it is *my* satisfaction that defines who God is.

This is an attitude toward God which is often implicit when the practice of religion is identified with "getting to heaven," seeking ultimate satisfaction and thus escaping ultimate punishment. "Keeping the rules" will be the whole name of the game, and the rules will be kept because they guarantee an ultimate reward. The *real* will· of God *for me* will not be distinguished on the whole from society's rules, because God himself is not differentiated from other agents or agencies that reward and punish.

This does not mean there is no objective sinfulness at this early level of consciousness. To return to an example I used before, a small child can smash a dimestore dinner plate in anger. That action is a genuinely disruptive action; however insignificant it may be, it contributes to the cosmic condition of moral disharmony which we have come to call "original sin."

But the child cannot yet distinguish between this action and that of *accidentally* breaking a stack of mother's best china plates—certainly a more "serious sin," given mother's impulsive reaction! To the extent that children's own interiority is not yet distinct from outer standards, children are not yet moral. Their morality is someone else's, not their own possession. The same condition can persist in the case of grownups who observe a code which is understood to be God's law *simply because* someone else has said so.

The various attitudes I have been describing are not attitudes which we possess altogether or all at once at some stage in our lives. I have only wanted to characterize the *types* of attitude toward God, morality and the experience of sin which arise at the earliest stages of religious consciousness, and which can so easily persist into adulthood. It is important to recall how far the human race had to grow before one can really speak of *conscious* morality.

Look at the characters in Homer's *Iliad*—one of our earliest western literary treasures, but not all that ancient in terms of the history of the human race. The characters in the *Iliad* do not really *decide* anything. The beginnings of action, for Achilles and Hector and Patroclus and the others, are not in conscious plans, conscious reasons and motives, but rather in the speeches of gods. In every novel situation, a man in the *Iliad* hears a voice telling him what to do. These voices or gods start the war in the *Iliad,* they devise its strategy, they determine the outcome of every crisis. (I owe this insight to an unpublished paper by Julian Jaynes.) *Conscious* morality, the awareness of freedom and each person's responsibility for the human situation, appears relatively late in human history and does not yet seem to be explicit in so late a document as the *Iliad.* Nor is such an awareness easily sustained. The gospel tries to foster it, but the gospel's level of awareness is not easy to accept.

As consciousness develops, human persons become gradually aware of their own autonomy. They begin the long process of distinguishing their own interiority from the outside world. This opens the way to a more personal idea of God, who is no longer identified with natural processes and who becomes distinct from other forces and authorities operative in human life. Fear gives way to love, and one's notion of love develops beyond the infantile desire for satisfaction. We become aware of our own potentialities, but we have not yet discovered them within *ourselves.*

We first observe our own potentialities in others, in heroes and heroines, in persons who embody some ideal. It is these heroes and heroines, projections of our own interiority, who motivate our search for our own individual personhood. At this stage the enforcing God gives way to a more personal loving God; and for the Christian, the figure of Jesus becomes the ultimate hero, the perfect embodiment of love for God and humankind.

The moral conscience here undergoes a significant development. Morality becomes much less a matter of observing a set of fixed commandments for fear of punishment or for the sake of a reward. A loving God has entered into a covenant with his people, and he remains faithful even when his people are sinful. Sin is therefore no longer the violation of a mysterious and undifferentiated system; it is an offense against a loving God. The experience of sin is much less an experience of defilement felt in the presence of a kind of harmful substance. Sin is now a violated relationship. And the symbolism of sin shifts from the language of "stain" and "uncleanness" to that of "turning away" from God, "rebellion" against God.

Still, the process of interiorization, the process of becoming conscious is not yet complete. At this stage of development, which I call the stage of "idealization," there is an awareness of the objectivity of sinfulness and inadequacy in us and around us. Sin is the *violation of an ideal,* and I feel the distance between myself and a loving God. But exactly how is this ideal to be reached? *Can* it be reached? How far does my *personal* responsibility go? And to what extent am I *subjectively culpable* insofar as I *don't* live up to the ideal?

Such questions are not really answerable. Ideal virtues, ideal norms are still abstractions. The ideals we see represented *outside* ourselves—in our heroes, in other people—look quite different from the way they look whenever we have managed to realize or concretize them to any degree *within* ourselves. One must go on to ask, "What is it possible for *me* to be? What are *my* inner resources? What are *my* concrete potentialities, given my failures and successes as a person up to this moment?"

To grow beyond idealization means to come to

terms with other people as subjects in their own right, not as representatives of our own projections. This includes God, who must also finally become personal —no longer an enforcer, not even a representative of ideal love, but someone to be struggled with and discovered in the midst of human experience and one's own search for personhood. It is only when we go beyond idealization that we come to know other people in a really personal way. A personal relationship between any two people is formed through all kinds of conflict, give and take, mutual trade-offs and psychic bargaining; all of this is needed for two people to become real to each other and not just ideal.

God, we believe, is a personal love who stands by us. He does not keep us from having to endure things; rather, he is a personal love who is there for us no matter what we have to endure. But our relationship with this God, if it is an adult relationship, will be subject to all the experiences of struggle and search and discovery that exist in any other *personal* relationship. God here will be the kind of God with whom Jacob wrestled, the elusive stranger whom Jacob never succeeded in pinning down, not even with a name. And the ancient story tells us—with a touch of humor which is also a stroke of timeless spiritual insight—that as a result of the encounter, Jacob limped for the rest of his life (Gen. 31:23–33).

Encounter with God led Jesus to accept death, confident that the Father's faithfulness to him would reach beyond death. This event made way for a shocking sort of humanism in which love for God was no longer to be a distinct thing from love for one's neighbor. The connection here is by no means an obvious one. It was not obvious in the ancient world, not even in Judaism, a very advanced state of religious awareness. In Jesus' time, late in human history, love for God was associated with distinct religious observances and religious practices that were often little related to service given to one's neighbor. And there are those who speak of Sunday worship as "giving one hour a week to God," as if the rest of the week were not given to God, or as if that hour were not also an hour given to one's neighbor.

We tend in many subtle ways to create separate categories for "religious" duties and "secular" duties, and to this extent we miss the import of the new commandment. The followers of Jesus are to love one another as God loved the world in sending his son. This love for one another is a revelation to the world, it reveals God himself to the world, it reveals God's presence *in* the world, to such an extent that the followers of Jesus will perform even greater works than he (Jn 13:34–35, 14:12, 17:21–23).

At the core of Christianity lies the belief that God's self-revelation in Jesus is so total that God is not to be sought outside this world, outside our most concrete human experience, nor even in the temples of this world. He is to be found first in the temple of our hearts, in our own personal histories, not in shrines of stone nor in the monuments of fixed ideas, but in the living flesh, in the same human experiences that Jesus himself endured. It is terribly inadequate to speak of Jesus Christ as the God-man. This idea hyphenates divinity and humanity. It splits into two and creates a tension between realities which Christian faith insists are resolved and integrated in the man Jesus. In just the same way, insofar as we separate the sacred from the secular, religious duties from ethical and human duties, we are departing from the "new morality" of the gospel.

In the light of the gospel, our usual definitions of morality and sin and goodness—including the definitions we often teach children—are shockingly inadequate. At the stage of consciousness which the Christian is asked to deal with, morality involves accepting responsibility for oneself. Morality is no longer an abstract ideal, and the question "What does God demand?" becomes the frighteningly concrete question "What does God want *of me?*"

Sin in a fully personal and adult sense is thus something other than the violation of an abstract ideal, and something more than the experience of an infinite distance between oneself and a loving God. At any point of our lives such a distance will be felt, sometimes very strongly felt, insofar as we have not yet actually become what we slowly realize we *can* become and are *called* to become—you in all your particularity, I in mine. As we grope our way toward God and toward realization of ourselves, we undergo the type of experience described by Paul in Romans 7–8, the experience of a radical inability to bring our total psyches into accord with what the conscious mind wills. It is in this experience of weakness and inadequacy and disorientation that we cry "Father!" —in the faith and trust that the Spirit of God will bring fruit from what we can see as only barrenness.

But isn't this essentially the same cry which the evangelists tell us Jesus uttered in the garden of Gethsemane? Sin is not the experience of being inadequate or weak. That is only the objective condition of humanity which we all share in varying degrees, depending on how we have developed or failed to develop our own interior resources.

What then is the experience of sin at a thoroughly adult level? The difference between your inner resources and mine, both of us much affected by the failures and successes and half-conscious events of our past histories, makes it impossible to give a definition in the usual sense of the term. The experience of sin as a fully subjective event, an event in which we discover ourselves culpable, might be described as the *failure to accept responsibility for our own humanness.* This is not an ideal or abstract responsibility: all of us can ideally become more than we are now. Sin is the failure to be responsibly human in concrete situations where, knowing that our limited resources are needed, we decide not to bring them into play.

Let us reflect on this thing I have called "humanness." Unfortunately I can't define it for you, because there is no ideal abstraction, no abstract definition which I can lay before your *minds* to explain what goes on in your *selves,* or in my self. Humanness is something that can only be symbolized, and we use symbols precisely because symbols are our means of pointing to something that remains undefinable, something that always remains essentially unknown, essentially mysterious. Our egos, our conscious psyche, that part of our psyche which is only the tip of an iceberg, demands clarity. Becoming human and pursuing humanness asks for the abandonment of clarity, the kind of clarity the ego seeks, the kind of clarity which comforts me and allows me to think that all I really am is what I *think* I am, and that's all there is to it. The ego wants clarity, and if we live only on our egos, if we live only on the tip of the iceberg which is our total selves, we will not want to enter into the real mystery of ourselves. We will not want to discover what Jung calls the Self, that second personality within ourselves which is not the conscious ego.

The Self, once again, cannot be defined; it can only be symbolized. If we use bread and wine and water to make real to ourselves the mystery of Jesus, so too we can only use symbols to point to the mystery which is ourselves. So let me throw a few symbols your way.

To pursue humanness is to go into the tomb with Christ Jesus and join him in death, so that we might live a new life (Rom 6:4). To pursue humanness is to go into the tomb which is the mystery of ourselves, because it is only there that we finally discover what is the mystery of Jesus. Faith in Jesus is faith in an outsider until we have gone into the tomb which is the mystery of ourselves—a mystery which our conscious egos like to resist because our egos want clarity. But *true* clarity about ourselves often comes out of experiences of death, experiences in which we are drawn into the darkness of the tomb and learn that there is much more to ourselves than what we thought we were.

The people who surrounded Jesus all had clear and distinct ideas about what the messiah should be and therefore what he, Jesus, should be. Even John the Baptist, as Matthew depicts him, was puzzled and troubled at Jesus' conception and execution of his messianic mission. All of this is ego-clarity, which involves living on the basis of fixed expectations, the expectations of others, even our own fixed expectations of ourselves. But Jesus did not live on ego-clarity. He pursued his own humanness, even to death on a cross, in order to answer the frighteningly concrete question "What does God want *of me?*"

It is only at this level, it seems to me, that one can make sense of the biblical idea that Jesus was "without sin" (Heb 4:15). No one who belongs to the finite human condition—not even the man Christ Jesus—is exempt from growth, from search, from the struggle of relating to others, from the gradual and painful discovery of what one is called to become. Christian faith holds that Jesus gave himself totally to this process. He did not "sin," he fully accepted responsibility for his own humanness, he did not stray from the path of becoming human, i.e. becoming everything God wanted *him* to be. This was the self-emptying, or rather the *ego*-emptying, the humble submission that saved him out of death and gave him the name which is above all names (Heb 5:7; Phil 2:7–9).

For Jesus, as I understand that man and meditate upon him, "sin" would have been the failure to give himself singlemindedly to the course to which he saw the Father calling him. Kazantzakis' novel *The Last*

Temptation of Christ develops this idea with extraordinary insight. Jesus, crucified and dying, undergoes his last temptation in the form of a dream. The dream shows him leading quite another kind of life, and the fantasy asks him to wish that he had taken a different course from the real one, the one that led to crucifixion. Jesus refuses the dream temptation, "keeping his word to the very end."

This is profound, and I think it is what the gospels emphasize in their own symbolic terms. You and I generally say, at good moments, "I do wish various things could have been otherwise; but yes, I'll accept what has happened and make the best of it." Kazantzakis is saying something much more about Jesus. In refusing the dream-temptation, Jesus, going into death, says this: "No, I don't wish it had been otherwise. I accept the whole works, I accept everything just as it has been, and I do not even wish anything had been different. This is where I belong, and this is where my life and preaching have brought me. This cross is *me.* For me to be anywhere else would be a failure to accept responsibility for *my* humanness."

One might say that Jesus reached the final and truest clarity about himself precisely at the moment of death. I think the Fourth Gospel says the same thing in its insistence that Jesus' death is at once his glorification, his exaltation, his return to the Father. Put it this way: Jesus' own final self-clarity comes in his being "lifted up."

An adult consciousness of being and becoming human transcends definitions. It can only be symbolized, and I have tried to suggest a few central Christian symbols which point to the mystery of our inner selves. Reach into your own experience to test my definition of sin as the "failure to accept responsibility for one's own humanness." I think we generally fail to appreciate the standard of morality reflected by some of the bible stories, which draw us way beyond precepts and commandments, clear and distinct norms of right and wrong. Adult Christian morality takes its cue from the widow of the gospel story who gives her last few cents to help others who might be in need (Mk 12:41–44), or from the widow who fed Elijah without knowing where her next meal would come from (1 Kg 17:10–16).

What the gospel asks us to do is to move out of that ego-concerned, ego-protecting, "ego-demanding-clarity" position, where we define in advance just what our resources are and where they end. Our ego-definitions are mostly unrealistic, and sometimes it is not until we offer the apparent last few cents that we realize just how much those few cents are worth —or even that we possessed them. The refusal to engage one's resources, consciously or only dimly known, can be the context in which the *experience* of sin becomes most real to an adult.

The Bible gives us no final definition of sin. There are practically as many descriptions or images of sin as there are writers (a fact which catechisms have generally overlooked). Honest and discerning reflection on our personal experience can tell us, as it told the biblical writers themselves, more about what sin is than what any "definition" ever managed to say.

The trouble is, we are not always so honest and

discerning. The psychic dynamics inherited from earlier stages of consciousness affect us more deeply than we realize, generating feelings of guilt coming from failures to live up to an ideal, or primitive feelings of uncleanness stemming from the violation of a system. (How do you *feel* when you cross against a red light, even if there is no traffic in sight?) But the human psyche is quite resilient, and it manages to absorb all sorts of feelings of sin, whether the sin is real or not. Our psyches can easily generate a kind of self-forgiveness, especially when as adults we are able to see beyond a God who would hold us to approved systems or to unrealizable ideals.

The question is whether self-forgiveness really works. Our consciousness always needs to be raised beyond defilement and beyond idealization, into a sense of what it is to become human. This is where rituals of penance and reconciliation have an essential role to play.

Chapter 4

THE EXPERIENCE OF RECONCILIATION

A number of the major characters in Graham Greene's novels are people who experience the depth of despair and desolation before new light and hope come into their lives. I remember reading one critic who posed this question of Greene's novels: Do you have to be lying in the gutter before you can experience the grace of God?

There is no law that says so. But isn't it often through the deepest experiences of darkness, or *out of* these experiences, that we come to realize most intensely what the grace of God means, concretely and experientially? This seems to be what Saint Paul is pointing to, in Romans 7 and 8: I find myself torn within myself; I find myself unable to do what I most want to do. Is there any way out of this mess? Thanks be to God, there *is* a way out. The way out is the life of the spirit, the grace of God, the spirit of God made known in Jesus.

But our experience of grace does not usually begin with the degree of maturity and self-awareness implied by Paul. What Christians call "grace" means quite different things at the different stages of consciousness which I outlined above. Permit me, in the following pages, to use the word "grace" in a loose and general sense to denote the opposite experience from that of sin.

FIRST STAGE: If the experience of sin at this stage is a *sense of uncleanness at being out of line,* the experience of grace here might be called a *sense of relief (phew!) at being back in step.*

This is the experience of being clean again, or ridding ourselves of the unclean substance that has been plaguing us. Penitential rituals first appear on the human scene as a means of coping with the experience of uncleanness. Primitive penitential rituals deal with washing or burning, driving away or spitting out, covering up and burying. But unless one has grown beyond this stage of consciousness, a penitential ritual will be liable to function simply as a rite of purification and thus reinforce a primitive, not-yet-Christian attitude toward sin. At times the notion of "reconciliation to the altar" has meant simply restoration to ritual purity.

This mentality has been implied when confession was used as a kind of purging of the week's impurities in preparation for Sunday's sacred activities, or when people have felt uncomfortable about continuing to receive communion because they haven't been to confession recently. Such attitudes reflect the ancient notion of sin as a kind of substance that haunts us, a stain that needs to be removed.

The use of such imagery in catechetics and preaching is highly questionable. "Stain" imagery is not prominent in the New Testament writings, which emphasize the social and ethical meaning of sin. Even with regard to baptism, the obvious symbolism of "washing away sin" is subordinated by writers like John and Paul to the much more sophisticated ideas of baptism into Christ's death, rebirth through water and the Spirit, new life, and the "love of God poured into our hearts."

I suspect that stain-imagery became particularly prominent in connection with the ritual of individual confession, as we have known it in the recent past. For many Catholics, the confessional became above all else a forum for handling matters of sexual purity, often with little differentiation between the biology or mechanics of sex and the morality of its use. Overemphasis on sex, on the part of both penitents and confessors, may have been fostered by an ancient psychic dynamic which associates *moral* purity with *physical and sexual* purity, leaving the two quite un-differentiated.

This regressive symbolism, which does not distinguish the physical from the moral, seems to have become associated with the ritual of confession. We all know that it is by no means easy to pinpoint the precise *moral* questions involved in the complex issue of human sexuality. But the confessional, for many people, identified the physical and the moral. Operative here, perhaps, was a primitive understanding of sin as "stains on the soul," coupled with an understanding of confession as a means of "purification" from those stains.

SECOND STAGE: If the experience of sin at this stage is a *sense of guilt at not living up to an ideal,* the experience of grace could be described as *a sense of renewed enthusiasm at being recommitted to the ideal.*

The problematic word here is the word "ideal." Ideals in themselves are *abstractions.* This is the difficulty with the stage of idealization, the stage where heroes and heroines represent the best of what is in ourselves—but not yet discovered *within* our own selves. At this stage, one can easily get locked into the depressing trap of attempting to live up to an ideal, and inevitably failing to do so. I can go to a retreat and get all psyched up on the ideal and recommitted to the ideal, but then I go home and fail as usual, only to go back to another renewal weekend and get re-psyched, fail again, and so on ad infinitum.

Ideals are important, and throughout our lives we always have to examine what our ideals are, what are the principles that govern our behavior. But as I indicated at some length earlier, there is a question that goes beyond ideals: Does God call us to live up to an ideal? Or does he call us to something much richer? You and I are human persons made up of successes and failures, sin and grace, uglies and beauties. In our individuality, we are much more beautiful than any abstract ideal. So the real question—and I think it is the gospel question—is this: Who are *you* called by God to be, you in all your individuality and I in mine?

It is hard for us to hear this question, because entirely too much preaching deals with laying out the Christian ideal and urging people to live up to it. This is preaching Christ the outsider, Christ the ideal projection, and it misses the real Jesus who always seemed to be telling people, in his own preaching: "No matter what good ideals you come up with, they are never enough. I have not come to abolish ideals, but to give you a greater challenge. You have to answer to God on the grounds of your own inner call, not on the grounds of outer ideals laid down by someone else." Isn't this the gist of the sermon on the mount? "Moses told you this, and the Law told you that. I tell you it isn't enough."

THIRD STAGE: The experience of sin at this stage involves the failure to take responsibility for our humanness, our being the way we are. The experience of sin here could also be described as a *sense of sorrow about one's brokenness.* This sorrow is different from guilt. Perhaps most feelings of guilt have to do with our failures to live up to other people's expectations of us—or to our own fixed expectations of ourselves, based on some abstract ideal. Sorrow is a deeper experience; it goes beyond idealization to realization of one's true brokenness, and a gradual acceptance of one's own individual humanness.

It is at this stage that the experience of grace finally becomes an *experience of reconciliation.* Reconciliation, first of all, with myself, with my being the way I am. And if I have accepted my own brokenness, I can have a new sense of what it is to be reconciled with others, accepted by others. I can even acquire the patience to wait, in those many instances when some other person is not ready to be reconciled with me. Finally, I can be reconciled with God, because at this stage I come to realize that God loves me *as I am,* in all my brokenness.

There is a fuller meaning to the word "reconciliation" than Catholics are giving it. I got a clue to this from a remark made by a parishioner one afternoon. "Father," he said, "I'm puzzled about something. We used to call this sacrament confession. Now it's called reconciliation. My problem is, I ain't mad at nobody." His remark reminded me of a huge pizzaria sign, "Opie Ain't Mad At Nobody."

Reconciliation means much more than the restoration of a deliberately broken relationship. Reconciliation is also the process by which people are called to realize wholeness. "Lord, I'm not finished yet" is much more than "I ain't mad at nobody." Is it possible that our failure to help ourselves and others to achieve wholeness is just as sinful as the overt and hostile severance of a healthy relationship? Let's look at some other possible kinds of reconciliation.

RECONCILIATION: SUPPORT AND ENCOURAGEMENT

A person who supports and encourages is an enabler. The enabler sees something good and beautiful in another person, something which the person has never been conscious or aware of. The enabler-reconciler helps other people to make a kind of passover from where they are to where they can be. The enabler-reconciler motivates, inspires, facilitates, and calls a person who may imagine he knows who he is to be reconciled and united with the person he really is.

High on the list of enablers in my life were my parents. Never did I hear them utter the seven last words, "We've never done it that way before." It was always, "Let's give it a try."

When I was eight years old, my father's sister gave our family her piano. I was in awe of this beautiful piece of furniture and my imagination was fired with the thought of the many possibilities this piano held out to me.

One evening after supper I went to the piano and picked out the notes to *Adeste Fideles*. My father sat down beside me on the piano bench and feigned astonishment. "Did you learn this all by yourself?" he asked. Proudly I told him that I had, and that I wanted to learn more songs. "Well," he sighed, "I don't have the money to give you piano lessons, but don't let that stop you, Jack. I think you are going to be a fine piano player, and no one in this house will ever stop you. All you need to do is give it a try."

Even though I practiced the piano four hours a day for the next ten years, music never became the main focus of my life. But it did become an integral part of my life. Had not my parents enabled me to discover this musical talent, I suspect that I would be less a person than I am. My father was a reconciler because he enabled me to surface and be united with a part of my true self I might not otherwise have known. Music helped me become more the person God created me to be. In that realized humanness, God's Spirit enabled Jesus Christ to live more fully in my life.

RECONCILIATION: FRIENDSHIP RE-VISITED

One Sunday afternoon I went to a nearby parish dinner. After I had seated myself at the table, I was introduced to a man sitting next to me. After we had visited for a few minutes, the man said to me, "Father, don't you know who I am?" Nervously I replied that I did not, and he tactfully reminded me that we were high-school classmates. In my embarrassment I suddenly recognized him and remembered that we had been very close friends. I told him that if I had been told on graduation day, 1940, that this would happen 37 years later, I would never have believed it. But it happened!

I once saw a greeting card which read: "He who ceases to be a friend never was one." Relationships which are taken for granted and not open for renewal are probably not healthy relationships in the first place. Isn't it odd that we never think of the renewal of friendships as a form of reconciliation? Physical proximity such as we experience in school, marriage, religious community, or parish life is no guarantee that relationships are growing. Even as we live physically together we must initiate new depths of our friendships as well as re-negotiate the old ones.

THE EXPERIENCE OF RECONCILIATION

Thirty-seven years of carelessness and inattention to a friendship between a former classmate and myself resulted in a brokenness that was so complete that I did not recognize him. Now I am wondering if our daily proximity in four years of high school was not a facade for the fact that perhaps we really weren't friends after all.

Is this kind of brokenness happening among people who live under the same roof, who live in the same neighborhood or parish? "I ain't mad at nobody" is no guarantee brokenness isn't there. The deepening and the strengthening of relationships is as much a prerogative of reconciliation as the reconciliation of repentant enemies.

This kind of reconciliation is nothing new in the Catholic Church. The Church has always encouraged us to pray often, to fast and abstain, to participate at least once a week in the Sunday liturgy, and to go to confession regularly. When we do these only out of a sense of obligation, we are missing the point the Church envisions. These are not mere obligations —paying, praying, and obeying in exchange for hatching, matching, and dispatching. In calling us to these duties (I do not hesitate to use the word duty), the Church is inviting us to renew our relationship with God, neighbor, and self, and at the same time, to deepen those relationships. How I am related to God now, for example, is not necessarily the fullest relationship I can have with him. Where I am now and where I can yet be is the work of reconciliation.

God does not necessarily give himself through rites, laws, and contracts. God gives himself through the interaction of relationships in a way that mirrors eternal and holy (wholly) relationships of the Father, Son, and Holy Spirit. Just as God is One in the interaction of these eternal relationships, so the Church is a sign and sacrament that the oneness of God can be mirrored in the oneness of humanity. Human relationships are not eternal, perfect, and whole. They must be fostered, strengthened, supported, attended to by human endeavor, and graced by the presence of God. Reconciliation is that human and graced endeavor.

RECONCILIATION: DISCOVERY OF RESOURCEFULNESS

We are a nation that has always prided itself on its independence. And yet, there are growing signs that we are becoming paralyzed by a dependency akin to addiction. When I talk about addiction I am not referring to chemical dependency. I am talking about the abdication of human resourcefulness. We have come a long way from the independent spirit of George Washington to the "let George do it" dependency of which chemical dependency may very well be a symptom. We seem to be situated somewhere between Pavlov's dog and George Orwell's 1984. Pavlov set in motion the salivary glands of consumerism which has sold us on the idea of turning our wants into needs. By 1984, inflation may not be our only worry. We can also worry about the energy barons, our big brothers, deciding whether the dog gets the meat or not.

A loss of resourcefulness is a form of brokenness. The Church is not a Church only of popes, bishops, and priests. The Church is a community of all believers. The Church is calling all men and women to share their talents and charisms responsibly so that the Risen Christ can be more fully revealed in this community of people we call the Church. To the degree that men and women refuse to offer their resourcefulness to the Church, or to the degree that this resourcefulness is unwelcomed by legitimate authority, the Church is diminished and ineffective in the world.

When I first became a pastor, I frequently heard questions like these: "Why don't they fix the roof? Why don't they fix the kneelers? Why don't they mow the lawn more often?"

I kept asking myself, "Who are the 'they' these people are talking about?" I weighed about 45 pounds more than I do today, but that hardly qualified me to be a "they." Were the "they" the Rosary Society? No, because some of these women were asking the same questions. Perhaps the "they" were the bishop and the chancery staff. Hardly, because there are nearly eighty parishes in the diocese, and the chancery staff can't be repairing leaky roofs and broken kneelers or mowing lawns for eighty parishes.

I was convinced that I had to have a "they." So I formed a parish council. I didn't know a thing about parish councils and I really didn't care. All I wanted was a "they."

But a funny thing happened. The "they" spoke of

the parish as an "it." "Whatever it needs, Father, you do it."

I was crushed! I was a pastor of an "it" and "they" wanted me to supervise "it." Glory be to God, I was a plant supervisor!

Well, time went by. The plant supervisor was supervising the "it" and "they" were glad to belong to "it."

One evening, the "they" gathered to discuss the "it." I mentioned that five dead elm trees on the parish property needed to be cut down. I reported to my "they" that the lowest estimate for the tree cutting was $75.00 a tree. The "they" winced. Then came the moment of truth. One of the men said, "Why don't WE cut them down?"

The "they" became a "we" and what we did was cut down five "its." After that, a "we" parish began to move from a position of *belonging* to the Church to one of *being and doing* Church. The "it" was really a "we" and there was no "they" after all. Best of all, I was no longer a plant supervisor.

Church is verb as well as noun. The pastor is not the only verb in the parish. Everyone in the parish churches the Church. A pastor pastors best when he enables his people to become conscious of their great resourcefulness. Ministry does not flow out of holy orders. It flows out of baptism. When our parishioners moved from the "it" and the "they" to the "we" idea of parish, they were reconciled to a whole new understanding of themselves and their relationship to the Church. After that they became reconciled to the changes they once thought were so stupid when they regarded their Church as a "they" and an "it."

RECONCILIATION: I AM LOVED FOR WHO I AM

True reconciliation is unconditional and is based strictly on the dignity of who I am rather than on conditions I must fulfill before I can be reconciled. The reconciliation of the prodigal son to his father is just such unconditional reconciliation. The father paid no attention to his son's plea to be accepted back as a servant. He needed no more servants. What he desired was the return of a lost son. Despite his son's debauchery, the father loved his son more than all of his servants put together. How could a loving father celebrate the addition of one more servant? Servants come and go. They are easy to hire and easier to fire. But it is not every day that a beloved son, especially a lost son, returns to his father.

How surprised the son must have been! The reconciliation was far deeper than he imagined. The son had not only been welcomed back into physical proximity with the father, but had been reconciled to full filial relationship with him. It was as if the son had never left home at all. Not one word about the young man's spree was mentioned. All was forgotten, erased, blotted out. And why? Because the father loved his son just because he was his son. Uppermost in the father's mind was the relationship restored, not the money squandered, the embarrassment suffered, nor the anxiety borne.

What a priceless gift we give to others when we love them as they are and not as *we* would have them be. It is a priceless gift because we give to others the opportunity of discovering their true selves. To be reconciled to one's self brings about the wholeness wherein peace, joy, and genuine self-assurance are experienced, enabling the beloved to see life and beauty as they are.

RECONCILIATION: A PLEA FOR APPRECIATION.

Brokenness often occurs when people take each other for granted and lack appreciation for one another. To "appreciate" means to place a price on another. Sometimes I think we place a higher price on the pets we harbor and the things we own than the people we love.

Much to my sadness, I discovered only two days before my father died that our relationship could have been richer had I shown more appreciation for his fatherhood throughout my life.

A few days before he died, my father asked me, "Jack, have I been a good father?"

There is no way under heaven I can describe my remorse at that moment. It dawned on me that I had never told this simple, loving, caring, faithful man that I loved him and that I cherished him. In that one moment, all that he was, all that he meant to me became present. It was then that he became more fully my father and I became more fully his son. What happened was a reconciliation, not out of hostility, estrangement, nor alienation, but out of appreciation. I deeply regret the failure to tell my father frequently of my appreciation for him, not only because he would have enjoyed hearing it from me, but also because it would have nourished and made better an otherwise good relationship. Marital, parental, and filial relationships are renewable and must be frequently renewed if the wholeness of these relationships is to be realized.

What has persuaded husbands and wives that the commitment they verbalize at the altar need never be verbalized again? Is there some constitutional prohibition against parents speaking their appreciation to the children or children speaking their appreciation to the parents? Are these familiar omissions of appreciation at least partially responsible for much of today's marital and family brokenness?

To appreciate carries with it the connotation that there are those in our life who come first. We hold them in highest esteem; there are none we prize higher or value more dearly. So appreciation is not the routine gratitude we offer waitresses, service-station attendants or department-store clerks. And yet I dare say that I have routinely thanked these people far more often than I have appreciated the people I deeply prize and esteem and who are so indispensable to my life. "You always hurt the one you love, the one you shouldn't hurt at all," go the words to an old song. There are many ways to hurt our loved ones, and one of the worst is to take them for granted.

One afternoon I walked into our parish church and found the entire first-grade class kneeling in prayer around the altar. I knelt down with them, closed my eyes, and began to pray. After a few moments I became aware of a presence standing before me. I opened my eyes and looked straight into the eyes of a little boy. Grinning from ear to ear he blurted out, "Father I love you." And then without warning he planted on my cheek the biggest salivary kiss you can imagine. I was filled with joy, and I wanted to tell the whole world what a "wholly" feeling that little boy had just given me.

But more than that, this little fellow gave me the opportunity of experiencing the joy my father must have felt when on his deathbed I told him how much I appreciated his fatherhood.

RECONCILIATION: AUTHENTICITY

I am not a nostalgic person. But I have in my possession several objects from the past which serve as symbols of values I prize highly. One of these objects is a radio. For me it symbolizes authenticity.

The first radio I remember in our home was one my father made. It worked very well and was certainly a great improvement over the crystal set he had also made.

While the homemade battery-powered radio was adequate for our entertainment needs, the whole thing could have been described as "organized debris." Situated on a table in the dining room, it resembled little more than a pile of tubes, coils, wires, batteries, and knobs. My mother never quite accustomed herself to this latest work of my father's inventive genius, and she began to insist on a commercial radio, if for no other reason than her sense of decor.

In 1932, three years after my father launched his Rube Goldberg do-it-yourself model, he reluctantly purchased our first and only commercial radio. Unlike the homemade model stuck in a corner of the dining room, this 1932 Crosley was enshrined in the living room for all to see and hear.

There was never another radio purchased by my parents for the home. Today, almost half a century later, this radio continues to perform as well as it did the day it was purchased. Except for the replacement of a few tubes, it has never needed a bit of repair. As I said, it symbolizes for me the meaning of an authenticity which, I remember, characterized the times in which it was purchased.

In 1932, most Americans had very few possessions and even less money to buy what products were available. Our Crosley radio cost $29.95 and we were able to purchase it only after saving pennies, nickels and dimes in a glass jar for over a year. However, I have never lamented what we didn't have in those depression years. As a matter of fact, what we did have so far overshadowed what we didn't have that I feel we were greatly blessed. Our 1932 Crosley radio witnesses to some of those blessings—authenticity, genuineness, and pride of workmanship.

Ironically, a friend of mine recently purchased a plastic radio resembling the early 1930 models. It too sold for $29.95. On the very day it was purchased he had to return it to the store because it didn't work. The clerk handed him another one without question.

My friend asked him: "How do I know this one will work?"

"You don't," the clerk sighed, "you just return it until you find one that works. What do you expect for $29.95?"

In 1932, my parents could expect that for $29.95, the product they bought would work. Forty-seven years later, we proceed on a trial-and-error basis until we find something that works. In 1932 we had very little money but lots of authenticity. I still have a radio to prove it. Not quite fifty years later we have lots of money but very little authenticity.

When we talk about reconciliation, we must address ourselves to a kind of betrayal which has pervaded our national life and consciousness since, let's say, the assassination of President John Kennedy. I do not say the assassination began the betrayal—it exposed it. When it began I do not know, and perhaps I am only kidding myself when I speak of the authenticity of the Thirties. A well-built 1932 radio may have been the last vestige of a dying authenticity.

What I do know is that we are living under a depression of another kind. Today's depression finds us bereft of authenticity. Rip-off is the name of the game. If America died today its tombstone might read: "America, R.I.P.-Off." Nineteen sixty-three may be an arbitrary date and I won't argue or belabor the point. Since 1963, however, Americans have been acting like a people who are gradually surmising they "have been taken." Let's look at the record.

We have witnessed three major assassinations, several assassination attempts, a war in Vietnam originally billed as America's noble effort to keep Southeast Asia free from communism (the irony of it all), a seemingly endless list of corporation and congressional scandals, and Watergate. Deceit, cover-up, break-in, dirty tricks, hired prostitution in the sacred halls of Congress, corporation bribery, price-fixing, shoddy workmanship in return for inflated prices— these are the names of the game.

It would be the height of naivete to suggest that the recovery of authenticity will be accomplished on the levels mentioned above. You will never recover authenticity by writing new ethics codes for lawmakers, tightening inspection procedures to insure quality production, or enacting new legislation to protect the consumers. These steps are necessary not to make us authentic, but to make us conscious that we have lost the sense of authenticity. A man who will say to a customer, "What do you expect for $29.95?" has long since lost a sense of authenticity. When a store clerk routinely makes a statement like that (and his number is legion), can you not ultimately expect a president of the United States to cover up a break-in?

Where do we begin to recover a sense of authenticity? I'd say we begin by recovering a sense of justice. To the degree that we permit unjust attitudes toward others to form and nourish our personal values and priorities, we spawn a national rip-off eventually yielding fruit a hundredfold, extending even to the oval office of the highest position in the land.

Reconciliation can never be a reality as long as I justify unjust attitudes towards others. When I measure authenticity by the aggressiveness I exercise to achieve personal success, comfort, and security, at the expense of justice to others, I open the door to a massive bag of dirty tricks and the consequent assassination of authenticity.

Though it still performs well after nearly fifty years, the Crosley radio, I am sure, will someday wear out. But, as long as it works, I still have hope that the day will come again when for $29.95 I may expect a product to last for more than 24 hours.

Chapter 5

A BROADER UNDERSTANDING
OF SACRAMENT

History has important lessons to teach us, and the history of sacramental penance is no exception. As we look at our new rites, there are two mistakes in particular that we need to avoid, both of them illustrated by our past history. One is the trap of legalism; the next chapter will take up this problem. The other is the problem of having too narrow a view of what a sacrament is.

The work of this chapter will be to look at the early Church's way of celebrating forgiveness, and so to recover a broader understanding of the sacrament of penance.

The forgiveness of sin is central to the message of Jesus. It would take pages to list all the New Testament texts in which the announcement of forgiveness appears. But the New Testament gives us little help on the question of a "sacrament of penance" as we know it. Most Catholics probably associate that sacrament with the famous text from John's gospel. It was Easter evening, and Jesus appeared in the midst of his frightened friends:

> "Peace be with you. As the Father has sent me, so I send you." Then he breathed on them and said, "Receive the Holy Spirit. If you forgive men's sins, they are forgiven them; if you hold them bound, they are held bound" (Jn 20:21–23. NAB).

To a Catholic, the text seems clearly to be saying that Jesus commissioned the apostles to forgive sins through the sacrament of penance; and the apostles were empowered to pass on this authority by ordaining successors. But to someone who does not come out of the Catholic tradition of recent centuries, and who therefore reads the text with different presuppositions in mind, John's words say no such thing. They refer only to *baptismal* forgiveness. Or they refer to the *preaching* of forgiveness, and the text has no special sacrament in mind. Nor do the disciples represent only the hierarchy or the ordained ministry; they are symbolic of all disciples of the Lord.

These various interpretations, Catholic and otherwise, all illustrate how we need to distinguish the *theology* of forgiveness from the various *forms* in which the forgiveness of sin has been expressed in the course of Christian history. The interpretations I have just mentioned are all hemmed in by post-biblical and even post-reformation preoccupations. They have too many implicit restrictions in them: John means *only* this and *not* that. The text of the Fourth

Gospel is in fact silent about the specific forms in which the author or his readers understood the commission of Jesus to be exercised or ritually expressed by the faith community. In this text, the resurrection of Jesus, the gift of the Spirit and the Church's mission to the world are intimately tied up with the ministry of proclaiming forgiveness.[3]

What this evokes is the very basic Christian experience—the experience of Christians in any era—that life in the Spirit and hope for the future begins with healing, with forgiveness of a past which can so easily immobilize us and cripple the future. But John's text says nothing about the *shape* of the Church's ministry of proclaiming forgiveness. That ministry has had many shapes in the course of Christian history. (I shall deal only with the question of post-baptismal forgiveness.)

One shape is suggested in the gospel of Matthew, in a chapter where Jesus addresses his disciples on the subject of community discipline and mutual correction.

> If your brother should commit some wrong against you, go and point out his fault, but keep it between the two of you. If he listens to you, you have won your brother over. If he does not listen, summon another, so that every case may stand on the word of two or three witnesses. If he ignores them, refer it to the Church. If he ignores even the Church, then treat him as you would a gentile or a tax collector. I assure you, whatever you declare bound on earth shall be held bound in heaven, and whatever you

> declare loosed on earth shall be held loosed in heaven (Mt 18:15–18).

A much later age would find it practical for a sinner to confess serious offenses in the confessional and do penance in the manner assigned by a priest. Not so in Matthew's community, where there were various stages in the procedure of reconciliation. The "Church"—the community and its official representatives—did not become involved in the process until the divisiveness created by sin could no longer be dealt with privately between one Christian and another. In Matthew's community—to use a later terminology—*private* confession was *lay* confession. If and when the Church and its ministers became involved, the "sacrament of penance" was no longer private.

Another shape of the ministry of forgiveness is described in the epistle of James.

> If anyone among you is suffering hardship, he must pray. If a person is in good spirits, he should sing a hymn of praise. Is there anyone sick among you? He should ask for the presbyters of the Church. They in turn are to pray over him, anointing him with oil in the Name (of the Lord). This prayer uttered in faith will reclaim the one who is ill, and the Lord will restore him to health. If he has committed any sins, forgiveness will be his. Hence, declare your sins to one another, and pray for one another, that you may find healing. . . . The case may arise among you of someone straying from the truth, and of another bringing him back. Remember this; the person who

brings a sinner back from his way will save his soul
from death and cancel a multitude of sins (James
5:13–16, 19–20).

This passage includes the earliest description of
what we know as the sacrament of the sick. In
James's community, the liturgical function of anointing was assigned to the presbyters or elders. But note
that this description appears in the much larger context of communal prayer, confession to one another,
and the effort to bring sinners back to the community.
Forgiveness of sin is here part of the total ministry of
healing and reconciliation, and James's emphasis
falls on the role of the *community* in this ministry,
not just the community's leaders or ministers. Confession of sins belongs to this *communal* context.

The exhortation to "confess your sins to one another" may refer to the kind of liturgical action mentioned in the *Didache,* another of our earliest Christian documents, which urges the faithful to "confess
your faults in the assembly, and do not come to your
prayers with a bad conscience."[4] Communal admission of sin is here seen as a necessary preparation for
effective prayer and worship. The same idea is evoked
in the sermon on the mount: "If you bring your gift
to the altar and there recall that your brother has
anything against you, leave your gift at the altar, go
first to be reconciled with your brother, and then
come and offer your gift" (Mt 5:23–24).

This is a good point at which to ask a very post-
biblical question. Are these different practices of first-
century communities "sacramental"? The answer

clearly depends on what one means by "sacrament." Today's Catholic has been taught to understand that term largely in its medieval sense, in the sense summarized in various decrees of the Council of Trent. "Sacrament" in this sense refers to certain peak rituals, rituals which the faith community has come to understand as most central to the lives and needs of its members, most central to its celebration of the newness of life given through faith in Jesus.

This is a thoroughly legitimate understanding of the sacraments, but it by no means exhausts the meaning of *sacramentality*. The Church teaches that there are seven sacraments; but the Church has never taken the position that only these specific rituals are genuinely sacramental. Before the age of medieval scholasticism, there was a much broader understanding of "sacrament." During the era of the Church fathers, the term referred to the whole mystery of salvation, the gift of redemption through Jesus, and virtually any communal rite which celebrates that redemption. Augustine, for example, called the kiss of peace before communion a "sacrament" because this ritual gesture expresses something essential to Christian faith and the meaning of communion itself: How can you hold your heart back from someone whom your lips have touched?

There is a school of thought, much captivated with medieval developments, which looks upon earlier Christian understanding of the notion of sacrament (e.g. Augustine's understanding) as "vague" or as yet "undeveloped." This amounts to canonizing medieval theology, and contemporary Catholicism has had to correct this tendency in many areas. If scholasticism clarified certain elements in the Church's self-understanding, there were also severe losses during the middle ages, including a loss in awareness of the relationship of the sacraments to the Church as community. Today we need an understanding of sacramentality which takes better account of our *whole* tradition, and of an era which had a much richer ecclesial understanding than did the middle ages.

This is not an academic problem but a very practical one. We need to do away with the theological and psychological *distance* between officially defined rituals and other types of community prayer which in some way proclaim and celebrate our redemption in the name of Jesus. "Where two or three are gathered in my name, there am I in their midst" (Mt 18:20). A text like this talks about the presence of the Lord among his people and therefore about sacramentality. The text clearly indicates that whatever we say about peak rituals, their special importance and efficacy, we must not *oppose* peak rituals to those which are not recognized as such.

Let me illustrate. The eucharist is a peak ritual, a particular form of worship and prayer, an especially profound way of giving thanks to God, proclaiming the death of Jesus and the meaning of that death. I can also gather with a few friends to pray, to reflect on the meaning of my life and my faith, and direct my reflections to the Lord in whom we believe. This particular act of worship does not center around breaking the bread and sharing the cup, and it is not eucharistic. It does not use the signs of bread and wine which the entire Christian community recognizes as covenanted signs, signs which say to all Christians "Yes, with these signs we all know you are proclaiming the death of the Lord until he comes."

But is this gathering for common prayer *non-sacramental?* It is a different form of sacramentality, a different ritual expression of our common faith, of my life and that of the friends with whom I am praying. Our form of praying together has not been recognized by the Church, the larger community of faith, as an official form of proclaiming the Lord's death—and very rightly so, because the way my friends and I pray should not have to be a model for anyone else. But if our prayer is not a *sacrament*—a defined and universally recognized peak ritual—this does not make it any less *sacramental,* any less a ritual proclamation that faith in Jesus is our way to God.

I have emphasized this point because it is especially relevant to the question of the "sacrament of penance." The Council of Trent, which has shaped our modern understanding of this sacrament, did not know anything other than the ritual of privately confessing one's sins to a priest, who imparts absolution. The fathers of Trent wanted to affirm what they felt the reformers were denying, namely that the ritual of individual confession is an authentic expression of the Church's ministry of forgiveness. The issue in question was the sacramentality of one *particular* rite. Trent did not discuss the meaning of sacramentality in general, nor did it say that *only* private auricular confession is sacramental. In fact, the communities to which Matthew's gospel and James's letter were addressed did not know private confession as Trent knew it.

Nor did the first six centuries of Christians know anything of our modern practice.[5] There was the kind of communal confession referred to in the epistle of James and in the *Didache;* this was meant for every Christian. At the other end of the scale, and by no means affecting every Christian, was a penitential discipline for dealing with the type of situation described in Matthew 18—that is, serious and disruptive actions which so violated the Christian vision that they involved the drastic measure of exclusion from the community.

By the beginning of the third century, this discipline had come to be known as "second penance," and it was understood in relation to baptism. Just as one is baptized only once, so a person can undertake second penance, canonical penance, only once in a lifetime.

The shape of second penance varied from place to place, and there was no universal legislation governing the practice or the public ritual connected with it. Still, we can make some generalizations regarding the discipline. First of all, canonical penance dealt with offenses that were serious and indeed public—like murder, idolatry, adultery, apostasy, fraud, false witness. A much later age would consider many other offenses as subject to the penitential discipline: for example, it is seriously wrong to malign someone's reputation even outside a courtroom; one's business dealings can involve serious injustice apart from downright fraud; and protection of the family would one day extend to prohibition of all kinds of sexual minutiae. But during these early centuries, canonical penance was generally required only in the case of virtual *crimes* against the family, the community, or the faith of the Church.

The penances were strict, consisting of such things as fasting, curtailing sleep, wearing special penitential garb (goatskin) in public, not having marital relations, and even not practicing one's trade. Depending on the gravity of the offense, the period of penance could last for months or for five or ten or twenty years. In some cases lifelong obligations, such as permanent sexual abstinence, remained for anyone who undertook second penance. In effect, doing canonical penance meant suspending one's ordinary family and economic life. The idea here was that the Church community would support a penitent during the time of his penance, through almsgiving and prayer.

The ritual procedure for canonical penance was this: First the penitent would make a confession to the bishop, who would officially declare the penitent excluded from communion. Then would come the period of public penance, which had to be completed before one could return to communion. It was not until around 1000 A.D. that confession and absolution (by then a private rather than public procedure) were brought together into one action, so that a penitent could take communion before actually completing the time of penance.

The patristic discipline was clearly a pastoral flop. It is not surprising that by around the sixth century the formal procedure for second penance had come to be used less and less. The strictness of the discipline, together with the fact that it could be undertaken only once in a lifetime, made it impractical even for grave offenses.

One can also guess the effects which the absence of a more humane form of post-baptismal forgiveness had on eucharistic practice. If during this era people wanted to delay their baptism as long as possible, the baptized would also put off canonical penance, if it was called for, until the end of life. This undoubtedly contributed to the drop-off in communicants and to the laity's increasing distance from the eucharist. Even as early as the fourth century, we hear bishops complaining about the large number of people who take communion seldom or never.

But what about the more ordinary Christian during these six centuries, the dedicated and concerned Christian who did not get involved in the type of grave sin which called for canonical penance? Since there simply was nothing like the confessional, how did such a person understand the "sacrament of penance"?

During this era the forgiveness of sin was associated with a good many practices besides second penance, the formal canonical discipline. In the third century, for instance, Origen talks about the many ways in which sins are forgiven. There is the forgiveness that comes through almsgiving (a most important Christian practice in those days when there were no government-supported social agencies to help the needy). There is the forgiveness that comes through our forgiving one another, as we learn in the Lord's

Prayer. There is the forgiveness that comes when one converts a sinner from the error of his ways; or when one shows an abundance of love, like the woman of whom Jesus said "Much is forgiven her because she has shown much love."

Only at the end of his list does Origen mention the formal discipline of second penance, which one would apparently not undertake without the advice of a spiritual director.[6] Spiritual directors, who were not necessarily priests, were important in monastic communities and in some lay circles, where confession of sins was practiced as a form of spiritual therapy. This was not yet "private confession" in our sense. Such practices existed *alongside* the official canonical procedure which was allowed only once in a lifetime.

The penitential seasons were important for all Christians. Lent, Advent, and the ember seasons developed as periods when the entire community devoted itself to prayer, fasting and almsgiving in preparation for Easter and other major feasts. For Christians today, seasons like Lent, and Advent remain important occasions for taking account of one's Christian responsibilities; and in recent years emphasis has very happily shifted from "giving up" something for Lent to *taking on* something that will benefit people in need. Still, for us, the works of mercy have tended to belong to one realm of life, while the forgiveness of sin, absolution and the penance assigned in the confessional belong to another. We would not readily make the close connection between the *liturgical* and the *social-moral* realms which Leo the Great makes in one of his sermons to the people of fifth-century Rome.

> Sins are forgiven to the fullest extent when the entire church gathers to make a single prayer and a single confession. For if the Lord has promised to grant whatever two or three of his faithful together ask him, what will he deny to thousands of people who meet in one act of worship, making their petition together in one spirit?
>
> Beloved, it is a great and valuable thing in the Lord's eyes when all of Christ's people, men and women alike from every level of society, one in mind, gather together in worship and Christian duty; when a single purpose unites everyone in avoiding evil and doing good; when God is glorified in the deeds of his servants, and the author of all goodness is blessed in one great act of thanksgiving. The hungry are fed, the naked are clothed, the sick are visited, and everyone seeks not his own good but that of his neighbor, by making the most of his own means to relieve the misery of others.[7]

Leo does not give any details regarding the liturgical service here, but it is evident that we are dealing with a type of *community celebration of penance* associated with certain liturgical seasons. Leo's approach is remarkable for its refusal to place the effects of the sacraments and the moral behavior of the faithful in two separate categories. In his blending of the liturgical and moral domains, one could have no finer illustration of Vatican II's idea that the liturgy is meant to be "the summit toward which the activity of the Church is directed" and "the fountain from which all her power flows."[8]

Leo's text exemplifies the broader understanding of sacramentality which I mentioned earlier. During the era of the Church fathers, the only *canonical* penitential discipline—the only discipline understood at the level at which Trent later dealt with individual confession—was the rigorous public procedure known as second penance. But this was not the only procedure with which the *ministry of forgiveness* was associated. There is no doubt that canonical penance was regarded as what we would consider sacramental penance. But there is no evidence that anyone during this era would have considered the rites and practices existing *alongside* the canonical discipline as *nonsacramental.* It was not until many centuries later that the meaning of "sacrament" became restricted to defined canonical forms.

As I write these pages, in mid-1978, there is much concern among the hierarchy about general absolution, and the use of that sacramental form is hedged in by a variety of restrictions. This is probably a normal enough reaction. Caution seems to be the official order of the day whenever a new practice is instituted. Chapter 9 will return to the question of general absolution and communal celebrations of penance. For the moment, let me conclude with two remarks relevant to present and future practices.

(1) Communal forms of reconciliation and communal rites of forgiveness came first, centuries before individual confession appeared on the scene. This took place because of the Christian sense that *sacra-*

mental healing is first of all an *ecclesial* event, a process that centers around and engages the whole faith community. This is the sense that desperately needs attention today. Individual confession itself needs to recover this ecclesial meaning.

(2) The new rite distinguishes communal celebrations *with* general absolution from other penance services *without* absolution. But if one accepts the broader and older notion of "sacrament" outlined above, it is clear that *any* communal celebration of penance is in its own way "sacramental." Only a narrow legalism would fixate on whether or not words of absolution are uttered. A big challenge for the next generation of Catholics is whether we can overcome the legalism that became associated with the sacrament of penance.

Chapter 6

THE PROBLEM OF LEGALISM

Back in the days of the Reformation, in 1551, the Council of Trent wrote a decree on penance which defended the practice of confession against the attacks of various reformers. Yes, said Trent, confession is a true sacrament, and the Church has the authority of Christ to proclaim the forgiveness of sin in this form. Trent dealt with the doctrinal question, but its decree did not lead to the kind of liturgical revision which we now have before us. Trent did not address the question of the *quality and shape of the ritual itself.*

Vatican II took up the task that the Council of Trent left undone, and the *Constitution on the Sacred Liturgy* called for a revision of the rite of penance which would take account of questions like these: How do we make confession pastorally effective? How should the rite be structured in a way that will best meet the needs of the faithful? How can the sacrament become a genuine celebration of the mercy and forgiveness of God?

People's negative experiences of confession have been very substantially a result of what Trent left undone. One thing in particular has plagued the practice of confession, and that is *legalism.* Church law is good and useful; it is the community's summary of its wisdom and experience regarding the rights and responsibilities of membership in the community of faith. But laws are always the servant of the Church, never its master. So trouble arises whenever we see our relationship with God primarily in terms of observing laws.

Legalism came along to distort the Christian idea of the forgiveness of sin long before the Council of Trent. This chapter is the story of that development. It is an important story, with many lessons for today's Church: Can we come to realize that God's forgiveness does not follow the patterns of human justice? In our practice of sacramental penance, can we overcome the idea that the Lord's forgiveness is something we *earn?*

A distinct new phase in the history of sacramental penance began around the year 600 A.D. when Irish monks started coming to the mainland to evangelize the migrant peoples who had changed the shape of culture and society throughout Europe. The monks brought with them a custom which had developed back home out of the monastic practice of discussing one's interior life with another person (not necessarily a priest) and praying together for forgiveness.

The custom was undoubtedly shocking to many a good Catholic of the time; it was an unheard-of practice known as *individual confession,* and it took some time for the practice to be accepted. A penitent could confess to a priest, receive a penance from him, and finally absolution—not just once in a lifetime but as often as necessary. Many of the penances were still strict; one might have to spend a month or more living on bread and water for stealing a horse, or for starting a quarrel with a neighbor. But all of this could be handled privately with a priest.

There were obvious advantages here. This form of confessing privately was certainly more practical than the stern canonical procedure of earlier centuries. In fact, the old form of public penance, rarely practiced in the sixth century, virtually disappeared by the year 800 as a practice which one would ever voluntarily undertake. The old practice was undertaken only when one was compelled to do so, by reason of some serious public crime.

But if the new practice was more practical and humane, it also involved some serious losses. Penance became a purely private matter. The "body of Christ" was becoming a sacred host to be contemplated. The ecclesial sense of that body, the communal dimensions of forgiveness and the role of the faith community in the process of reconciliation were largely forgotten. These were the centuries when the Church more and more lost consciousness of itself as a *faith community* formed around the Lord's table, and became more and more a *legal organization,* an institution parallel to the state.

Moreover, during these centuries when society was reorganizing itself after the turmoil of the barbarian migrations, Church discipline virtually replaced civil law or was incredibly intermingled with it. Many signs of this appear in the "penitential books" used by confessors, volumes which assigned specific "tariffs" for specific sins. The sixth-century *Penitential of Columban,* for instance, sets a penance for homicide which is really indistinguishable from the sentence which would be imposed by the civil law of a primitive society. A man who kills his neighbor must do penance on bread and water for three years. He must then work for the family of the man he killed "and in his stead render filial piety and service; and thus after satisfaction has been made, let him be reconciled to the altar by the judgment of the priest." In the eighth and ninth centuries, people guilty of offenses like murder or perjury were kept in confinement from Ash Wednesday till Holy Thursday, the day when public penitents were reconciled to the altar.

Satisfaction for civil criminal offenses, in other words, became tied up with ecclesiastical supervision and canonical procedures. And in this rough and civilly disorganized era, the Church's ministry of forgiveness became thoroughly intertwined with a rugged society's manner of dealing with wrongdoers. We shall see later what effect this development had on the notion of "punishment due to sin."

Individual confession, as I mentioned earlier, developed out of monastic forms of spiritual direction and prayer. This sounds edifying enough. But it was a crude age, and neither the actions thought of as sinful nor the tariffs assigned as penances were always things that we today would locate in the category of "spiritual direction." Columban's penitential, for instance, contains this fascinating prescription for what another age would call "solitary sinners" and "dirty old men": If any monk, "desiring a bath, has washed alone naked, let him do penance with a special fast; but if anyone, while washing lawfully in the presence of his brethren, has done this standing, unless through the need of cleansing dirt more fully, let him be corrected with twenty-four strokes."

The connection between individual confession and monasticism was not entirely fortunate. The understanding was developing in those days that the monastery was the only place where the Christian life could be properly and fully lived in that rude world. So the penitential books carried around by confessors came to contain different categories of penances for clergy and laity. The *Penitential of Finnian,* for instance, imposes the following penance for one who has started a quarrel and plotted in his heart to strike or kill his neighbor: "If the offender is a cleric, he shall do penance for *half a year* with an allowance of bread and water; thus he will be reconciled to the altar." But if the offender is a layman, "he shall do penance for *one week,* since he is a man of the world; his guilt is lighter in this world and his reward less in the world to come."

This development of different standards of morality for different classes of Christians contributed still further to the breakdown of a sound ecclesial sense. We are moving further and further away from an awareness of the Church as a community united by a common faith, a community in which castes have no place.

Nor did the imposition of monastic-style penances help to make individual confession an integral or frequent part of the life of the laity. Between 800 and 1200, local ecclesiastical laws attempted to make confession obligatory once or twice or three times a year; regular confession was hardly a common or thoroughly voluntary practice. Finally, in 1215, a general council—Lateran IV—made yearly confession a general law of the Church. (It should be noted that this law, which is still a part of Catholic canon law, is tied up with the precept of receiving *communion* once a year. It is probably safe to assume, today as in 1215, that a Christian who communicates only once a year could profit from confession on that occasion. On the other hand, I have heard it argued that even the regular communicant is obliged to go to confession annually. This is not correct. Canon 901 makes it clear that confession is required by Church law only in the case of grave sin.)

Interestingly enough, as the *obligation* of periodical confession to a priest developed, greater importance came to be given to *lay confession*. If mortal sins were forgiven through confession to a priest, mutual confession among laypersons was understood as an ordinary means for the forgiveness of venial sins, that is, a non-canonical but nonetheless "sacramental" exercise of the ministry of healing. The custom was never widespread. As one might expect, lay confession was practiced only by spiritually mature Christians.

In one sense, "lay confession" is a gospel require-
ment for every Christian. We all need to reconcile
ourselves with people whom we have offended—and
this in a *personal* manner. It is a pity that absolution
in the confessional and the recitation of three Hail
Marys has so often given Catholics the impression
that we are thereby absolved from further efforts at
reconciliation.

A somewhat more formal kind of lay confession
could be a viable practice among Christians who are
interested in developing a personal sense of penance
and mutual reconciliation. Theologian Walter
Kasper emphasizes our need to restore this valuable
tradition of lay confession—which was altogether
lost, quite unnecessarily, after Trent's stress on the
value of priestly absolution had the effect of making
the confessional the *only* forum for devotional confession.

> The essence of lay confession is made up of three
> elements: (1) mutual conversion, which means tact-
> fully and wisely making one another aware of mis-
> takes, dangers and wrong attitudes; (2) the promise
> of God's grace, the word of encouragement in the
> Christian life, incitement to good and illustrations of
> how the Christian life can be realized; (3) interces-
> sion for the other and representative penance (i.e. a
> willingness to do penance on the other's behalf).
> Readiness to undertake the latter would be an unam-
> biguous way of distinguishing a self-righteous wish
> to criticize from a genuine *correctio fraterna* in

> which one is himself ready to do penance for the other.[9]

Once again, only a narrow understanding of sacramentality would exclude such a practice (how much more difficult than the confessional!) from the realm of what is, in a genuinely theological sense, truly sacramental: a few Christians gathered in reflection and prayer to celebrate their reconciliation with God through Christ Jesus.

How and when did the *priest's absolution* come to be understood as a key element in the sacramentality of penance? The question was not resolved during the first millennium of Christian history. Indeed, it was not even raised. It was understood that grave offenses (with varying understandings of the meaning of "grave") had to be brought to the attention of an ordained minister. But the precise role of the minister's absolution—his laying on of hands, or his verbal declaration of forgiveness—was not defined. And in the case of lesser offenses where the official procedures were not required, the *theological* meaning of the minister's absolution was quite indistinct from other forms of confession such as lay confession or, in the patristic era, community celebrations of penance.

As we move into the age of scholasticism, after the first millennium of Christian history, we begin hearing the statement that "penance is a sacrament." The term "sacrament" now begins to acquire the restricted technical sense that we moderns are familiar with. Granted that Christians celebrate their redemption in many ways, in many rituals: Which are the rituals that declare salvation in a manner independent from the holiness of the minister, from the esthetic quality of the ritual, from the immediate meaningfulness of the liturgical action? Which are the rituals most closely linked with the life of the Church, the rituals of which we can say "God's grace is certainly operative here"?

These are the questions which govern the whole medieval approach to sacramental theology. They are valid questions; and the answers given to them deal with what we know as the seven sacraments, seven specific rituals which were understood as covenanted signs to which the universal Church could attest, rituals in which the grace of Christ could be said to operate no matter what the human quality of the ritual might be. The medieval approach to the sacraments therefore dealt basically with those rituals which had gradually acquired universal canonical recognition as "peak rituals." Such recognition, which was shared by both the eastern and western churches, was based on a sound theological and liturgical sense.

But I must emphasize once again that medieval theology did not deal with anything *but* peak rituals. It did not deal with the question of sacramentality or with the genuinely sacramental character of *every* communal liturgical celebration.

Nor did medieval theology come to terms with the *relative importance* of the seven rituals, the subordination of one to another. Aristotelian concepts, the new learning of the day, came into play here. Aristotle's concepts were used to show what the seven sacraments had *in common,* not what was different about them. Sacraments, like rocks or plants or people, were understood as made up of matter and form. Penance was one of the seven sacraments; so penance had to have these elements in common with other realities. This analysis paid little attention to the actual historical origins of the Christian sacraments, most of which had been forgotten.

Theologians of this era did not in fact agree on what constituted the "matter and form" of the sacrament of penance. It was generally agreed that the interior acts of the penitent (sorrow for sin, confession, and the resolution to avoid sin) made up the "matter" of the sacrament. But what was the "form" of the sacrament? Albert the Great said that the form is God's grace; Albert attributed no special place to the priest's absolution.

It was Thomas Aquinas who first affirmed that absolution constitutes the "form" of the sacrament. As Thomas understood it, the acts of the penitent (matter) and the priest's absolution (form) make up a composite whole, with *both* aspects essential. But the matter-form analysis evolved still further. After Aquinas, Duns Scotus saw the priest's absolution (the form) as *essential,* and the interiority of the penitent (the matter) as only a necessary *condition* for receiving the all-important absolution.

Scotus won the day so far as subsequent Catholic tradition is concerned. His emphasis on the importance of absolution over the interior acts of the penitent made it possible for the catechisms of the following centuries to teach what most contemporary Catholics once learned: Sin can be forgiven through a "perfect" act of contrition without confession. But an "imperfect" act of contrition will suffice if one receives absolution in the confessional. Such a theory depends exclusively on the heavy value assigned to the priest's absolution by someone like Scotus. Aquinas could not and did not accept such a distinction.

But whether we are dealing with Aquinas or Scotus, we have to face the limitations of the medieval approach. Especially after Scotus, so much weight came to be placed on absolution that the sacrament of penance was bound to take on mechanical overtones. "Confession" in the biblical sense is an extremely rich notion; it means admitting one's inadequacy, one's poverty and need for God, a need for redemption from oneself and one's own selfishness. Undoubtedly there were people during the middle ages who profited from the spiritual therapy which individual confession could offer. But the theology of the day did not encourage sound practice. Medieval analysis of the sacrament was concerned almost exclusively with the minimal "essence" of the sacrament. Theological emphasis therefore fell on little more than the legal act of verbalizing a list of sins, the minimum requisite for receiving absolution.

This was the theology inherited by the Council of Trent. Trent had to cope with terrific abuses of penitential practice, including the whole matter of the sale of indulgences, pieces of paper which reputedly pardoned sins. The council wanted to reaffirm the authentic Christian tradition; but since the only tradition the conciliar fathers knew was the medieval one, their treatment of penance retains all the limitations of the medieval teaching.

One of the most striking weaknesses of Trent's theology of penance—the theology incorporated into the catechisms most of us used—is its individualistic tenor. Individual sins are forgiven through the absolution of the individual priest, who sets the private "satisfaction" that is to be done for the remaining "punishment due to sin." There is nothing in Trent about the communal nature of sin, the resonance of sin in the community of humankind, or the place of the Church as community in the process of reconciliation. Here as elsewhere, the lack of a sound *theology of the Church,* a defect shared by Catholics and Protestants alike in the sixteenth century, took its toll.

Another problem is the theological ambiguity connected with the notion of "punishment due to sin" and "satisfaction for sin." This ambiguity is noticeable not only in Trent but also in the canonical penitential discipline of the patristic era. In the course of the centuries, the Church's ministry of forgiveness became more and more tied up with society's way of coping with wrongdoing, so that *the penitential discipline became modeled on the procedures of human justice.*

In civil society, pardon is finally granted to a guilty person by reason of his "making satisfaction" for his offense, paying his debt to society for the wrong he has done. This is the model that has been implicit in the various canonical disciplines throughout Christian history. A sinner receives official pardon by reason of his making satisfaction for his offense. Even though his *sin* has been pardoned, he is not thought of as completely forgiven until full *satisfaction* is made, in this life or in the next. This is the point of view implicit in the whole notion of "punishment due to sin."

There is no doubt that Christians are obliged to make up for the wrong they have done. We have to make restitution, we have to reconcile ourselves with those whom we have wronged. And there is no doubt that we have to live with our mistakes. Sin leaves, if you will, a "personal remnant" in our characters which we have to cope with, a remnant which affects our inner resources and our future growth as persons. All of these elements have traditionally been included in the notion of "satisfaction for sin."

But the idea of satisfaction has also implied that God's forgiveness is *earned.* It is at this point that we have to reject the analogy with the procedures of human justice, or conceiving the forgiveness of sin on that model. We simply do not *earn* God's pardon. Apart from the idea of reconciliation with one's neighbor and coming to terms with one's own selfishness, there is, so far as I can see, no theological intelligibility to the notion of "punishment due to sin."

Just at the point where penance is thought of according to the model of *human* justice, it runs counter to the gospel idea of *God's* justice. God's forgiveness is total and free, given a change of heart on the part of the sinner. Insofar as Trent's approach to the sacrament of penance remains heavily legalistic, it fails to make this point clear.

I have been talking about weaknesses in Trent's over-all theological perspective, weaknesses inherited from medieval scholasticism and passed on to the catechisms and pulpits of our own day. But what about the Reformation itself? What were the theological arguments that occasioned the treatise on penance which has formed the basis for Catholic legislation, enduring up to the present?

Catholics and Protestants have often used confession as a touchstone for distinguishing themselves from one another. This was not the situation at the time of the Reformation. Luther, for instance, did not challenge the spiritual benefit of confession, nor did he want to get rid of this sacrament. Lutheranism eventually took another course; but Luther himself encouraged confession. He did object to distortions of the notion of satisfaction: "The best kind of satisfaction is to sin no more and to do all possible good toward your fellow man, be he enemy or friend. This kind of satisfaction is rarely mentioned; we think to pay everything simply through assigned prayers."

Any orthodox Christian would have to agree with this criticism. In any case, abuses of the sacrament did not affect Luther's admiration for "that most worthy, gracious, and holy sacrament of penance, which God gave for the comfort of all sinners when he gave the keys to Saint Peter in behalf of the whole Christian Church." The sacrament of penance brings about "forgiveness of sin, comfort and peace of conscience, besides joy and blessedness of heart over against all sins and terrors of conscience."[10] An essential part of the sacrament's comfort is absolution. "We receive absolution from the confessor as from God himself, by no means doubting but firmly believing that our sins are thereby forgiven before God in heaven."[11]

The problem at the time of the Reformation was not the practice of confession or receiving absolution, but rather the precise weight to be given to absolution itself. Luther had strong words to say about the idea that a ritual could be said to forgive sins or confer grace simply on the grounds that the penitent "places no obstacle" in the way of the sacrament. It is not the sacrament alone which forgives sins, but rather faith in the sacrament.

A number of the fathers at Trent defended essentially the same position, and they were not condemned for it. The council finally made a number of statements censuring anyone who would teach that *only* faith is efficacious, *not* the sacraments. But whoever might have been propounding this, it was not Luther's position.[12] In any case, when the fathers of Trent turned to the question of absolution, they insisted that absolution is a "judicial" act, not simply a "declarative" act which announces the forgiveness already granted through faith alone. Absolution, in other words, is an integral part of the process of sacramental reconciliation, not a mere appendage to it.[13] Again, whom is Trent censuring? Luther does speak of absolution as a "declaration" of forgiveness; but texts like the one I quoted above indicate that he certainly did not consider absolution an unnecessary appendage, a "mere" declaration.

Fortunately, historical study is enabling us to clear up many of the unhappy and unnecessary misunderstandings of the Reformation. I have brought up the problem of absolution only because it illustrates the difficulty I mentioned earlier: *Trent was unable to get beyond the theological limitations of conceiving absolution according to a legal model.* The Christian tradition had already sensed the inadequacy of this model, around the year 1000, by allowing absolution and reconciliation to the altar *before* the penitent had completed his penance—like a judge granting pardon before the criminal has served his sentence. But what is the meaning of the priest's absolution, and what is its relationship to the penitent's own interior conversion?

Medieval theology never resolved the question. Sometimes the interior and exterior, the private and the ecclesial elements of penance, were in balance, as in Aquinas. Sometimes they were only loosely related, as in Scotus. Trent did not advance the state of the question. By affirming that absolution is a "judicial act" in which the priest passes judgment and assigns satisfaction, the council simply used a legal analogy to affirm that absolution is a true part of sacramental penance.

This emphasis on the importance of absolution is only as good as the analogy on which it is based. Trent lacked an ecclesiology which would enable it to take the question of confession out of legal categories and locate absolution and the "power of the keys" within the larger ministry of reconciliation which belongs to the faith community as a whole.

For a Christian, to speak of God's pardon means to speak of the Church's mission to the world. The Church is a body called together by the Spirit of God in the name of Jesus for the purpose of making a unity among people. The vocation of any Christian community is to strive to appear before the world as a visible sign of peace and reconciliation. God's pardon, therefore, is not an abstraction; it is something which the Christian perceives and experiences in and through reconciliation and union with fellow Christians. Absolution is a proclamation, a "declaration" of the good news that reconciliation has taken place. This declaration is "judicial," that is, it is an official expression of the Church's mission of reconciliation. And the proclamation is made, whether communally or individually, to people to whom forgiveness *belongs* by renewed commitment to the gospel.

Our questions today are different from those of Trent, and the value of absolution is no longer the real focal point of the problem. Many Catholics have come to that same conclusion from reflection on their own lived faith experience. The real question is how we can fittingly *celebrate* the forgiveness that is always there for us. This is the question we shall now take up, as we look at the Church's new rites.

Chapter 7

CELEBRATING CONFESSION TODAY

When my mother died several years ago I discovered that she had designated me executor of her will. I had never been executor of a will and may the Lord deliver me from executing another one.

I soon discovered there was an immense amount of legality connected with this responsibility. My mother's will was a simple one, clearly stated, and easy to understand. Nevertheless, I had to execute it step by step according to very precise and detailed prescriptions of law.

One day, after a fifth trip to the lawyer's office, I vented my frustration with the complaint, "Why all of this red tape?"

The lawyer laughed and proceeded to enlighten me about "red tape" concerning wills. He began by appealing to my appreciation for the sacred. The state, he said, shows delicacy towards the intentions of the deceased. Laws are meant to insure that the will and intention of the deceased are executed as precisely and accurately as possible. Laws, he pointed out, are safeguards of one's will. They specify unjust actions people might take to violate the exact intention of the deceased. What is important, he said, is the sacredness of the deceased's will and the state's concern for that will. Laws safeguard this sacredness. They make sure that our attitudes and motives are consistent with the will of the deceased.

As I study and reflect on the revised rite of the sacrament of penance, I find the lawyer's explanation a good analogy to the spirit of the rite. I had approached confession with the same attitude as I approached my mother's will. I had let laws rob me of a tremendous experience of God's will, plan, and intention. I had been in awe of the frame and had missed the picture.

The lawyer's explanation changed a bad attitude in me. My mother's will was like a sacrament. It was a visible, concrete sign meant to enable her heirs to experience her love and generosity even after death. The laws concerning her will assured her, while living, that her love for us would be accurately expressed after her death. As executor, I had the peace of knowing that these laws protected the sacredness of her intentions. And finally, these laws brought to the beneficiaries the satisfaction that her will for them would be precisely and lovingly carried out.

The sacrament of penance is like a will. It is a visible, concrete sign of God's will, God's love, and God's generosity. It is meant to enable us, in faith, to experience the relationships of the Holy Trinity whose image our humanity mirrors. It is meant to make us aware that growth in God's divine life is in proportion to the ever deepening relationships with him and with all men and women. It is meant to renew the fervent last will and testament of Jesus when at the last supper he prayed "that they may be one as you, Father, are in me and I in you. May they be so completely one that the world will know you sent me" (John 17: 21). The sacrament of penance is visible evidence that the reconciling, unifying work of Jesus is continuing. He promised it, he wills it, he intends to execute it. His execution on the cross testifies to the firmness of that intent.

The work of the Church is to enable us to experience reconciliation and the peace flowing from renewed and healed relationships. The laws of God and Church are not what I confess to. They do not reconcile. They do not heal. They do not bring peace. They are there to identify sinfulness and the hideous consequences of damaged relationships which prevent God's reconciling, healing, and unifying work in our lives.

The sacrament of penance, like a will, is meant to enable us, God's children and beneficiaries, to experience the continuing love and generosity which he has promised. The sacrament is not the experience of laws. It is the experience of the living God and his forgiveness.

Have you ever spent time preparing a careful speech for the confessional box? I certainly have. I wanted to make sure I said all the essentials. But then again, I didn't want to say *too* much. Sometimes it was like getting ready for an appearance in court.

The Council of Trent insisted that sins should be confessed by number and kind. Just what did you do, and how many times did you do it? The council was calling for honesty and sincerity, and it was reacting against the practice of seeking absolution for no confession at all. People were apparently saying things like, "I have failed in my duties to God and neighbor"—period. Many were seeking sacramental forgiveness without any real desire to change their lives.

Unfortunately, the fathers of Trent wrote with the model of the courtroom in mind. As the last chapter indicated, Trent did not seem to be aware of the extent to which God's loving acceptance had become confused with human models of legal pardon. The council even spoke of the penitent as a "defendant." Their rule about naming and numbering one's sins was well intentioned, but it had the effect of fostering legalism.

The fathers of Vatican II were aware of this heritage of legalism. This is why they called for a new rite of penance which would express and celebrate the mercy of God, which is a much bigger and more loving thing than the pardon of a defendant in court.

Most of us grew up paying far more attention to *sins* than to sinful*ness.* Many confessors have had the experience of hearing a list of sins recited by a penitent, and suspecting from the whole tone of the confession that the list has little to do with what is really bothering the person. The list of *sins,* in other words, seems to have little resemblance to the penitent's real experience of sinful*ness.*

If the confessor asks, "Which of the things you

mentioned really matter to you, really affect your life?" he will sometimes get an answer like, "Well, Father, what really bothers me is this. . . ." And the penitent will go on to talk of a deeply felt experience of failure or inadequacy which simply doesn't fit into neat categories of number and kind.

In the past, the rite of confession has focused more on sins than on sinfulness, acts rather than attitudes. We came to confession often with symptoms, rather than the real disease. Individual acts are usually symptoms. This is not to say that symptoms aren't real. Sometimes they are very harmful indeed. But the real disease of sin most often stems from the half-conscious attitudes in which our freedom, or lack of freedom, becomes involved.

The new rite of confession picks up things that Trent left unsaid. The new rite is addressed to the disease rather than to the symptoms. Penitents are invited to "open their hearts" to the confessor, and the rite avoids the legalistic approach of asking penitents to list their sins by name and number. The rite takes account of the fact that sinfulness (the attitude) is not always the same thing as sins (the acts). It encourages us to bring our ambiguities and struggles to the sacrament, not just the clear-cut wrong things we have done.

So the new rite calls us to something more than the prepared speeches we have at times brought to confession in the past. Bringing a list of sinful acts (symptoms) is not always the same thing as opening one's heart and revealing a disease.

All of this calls for special qualities on the part of

the confessor. He should be a wise and understanding person who knows how to discern the workings of the Spirit of God in himself and in others. The qualities of the confessor described in the new rite suggest that hearing confessions is a special ministry, calling for special gifts and training.

As the new rite takes hold, it may become clear that not every priest is gifted for this ministry. Our bishops may have to do some serious thinking about appointing certain priests whose primary ministry would be hearing confessions, because of their particular gifts and call.

I remember boils!

For nearly a year of my adolescent life, I suffered a number of hideous, painful, volcanic boils. One morning I awoke feeling the first burning pain of a brand-new boil on the back of my neck. When I arrived in the kitchen where my mother was preparing breakfast, I didn't have to say a word. "Oh, no!" she exploded, "not another boil!"

There ensued a hasty conference with my father. "John," my mother declared in her very best General Patton manner, "we've got to get to the bottom of this boil business. I've had it with this kid!"

After school that day, I presented myself to our family doctor for another lancing session. This time, however, Doc Murphy "got to the bottom" of the problem. After some questioning about my eating habits, he determined that I not eat certain foods I had been eating too much of. "Too rich for your blood," he commented.

Well, he was right. I quit eating whatever the culprit was and the boils never appeared again. When Dr. Murphy quit lancing the symptoms and began to deal with the disease, I found lasting relief.

Confession has been a lot like this. It seems to me that the new rite of penance is saying, "Let's get to the disease and quit confessing boils." Just as boils are not the disease, so sinful acts are not the deeper and more rooted sinfulness of our lives. Have not our past confessions been mere lancing sessions? Penitents frequently complain, "Father, I keep committing the same sins over and over." Their complaint has the ring of disillusionment, and small wonder.

The basic disease, the fundamental sinfulness of each person is the failure to grow into the person God created him or her to be.

Human creation is not an assembly-line operation with God. When God created me, for example, he had someone specific in mind. He meant that I should grow toward that precise, explicit, and specific person I really am. My sinfulness is the failure even to ask, "Who am I called to be?" My sinfulness is the failure to take responsibility for my humanity so that incarnationally God can be who he is in my unique though limited self.

Does human responsibility for human growth exclude God's grace? Not at all! It is a condition for it. How else can we understand the beautiful teachings of the Church on Mary? Mary was sinless and because of her sinlessness was able to respond as fully as possible to God's call to be the mother of Jesus. Humanly, she was in possession of herself. God could "proclaim the greatness" of himself in her precisely because she knew that he "looked upon his lowly handmaid." Because she was sinless she was spared the delusion of an inflated ego. With poor "I"-sight she was able to perceive clearly the graciousness of the Father inviting her humanity to God. Sinfulness is the lie that I am the center of the universe, that no one can tell me what to do, and that all of life revolves around me. At the root of every sin is pride, and if you notice, "I" is at the center of that word too.

The new rite of penance is after attitudes rather than sins. It suggests that we examine the disease rather than lance boils, or if you like, to go for the jugular vein of sinfulness rather than the arteries of sin. If it becomes a mere rearrangement of furniture, it will fail to be an instrument of renewal and may do more harm than good. Reconciliation rooms, scripture readings, new prayers, and face-to-face confession, without the changes of attitude these things point to, will produce as little cureable and healing effect as moving a terminal cancer patient from a dark room to a lighter and more cheerfully decorated room.

Let us look at some of the features contained in the pastoral introduction to the new rite.

Confession is a celebration of God's mercy, not a court of judgment. From the moment when the confessor welcomes the penitent, to the concluding prayer of praise and thanksgiving, it is inescapable that we are dealing with a new atmosphere, an atmosphere of healing and prayer. The rite in fact insists that the priest as well as the penitent should prepare themselves by prayer to celebrate the sacrament (#15).

The story of the prodigal son is helpful in understanding the atmosphere of the new rite. The repentant son had a speech all prepared; it was a sincere speech in which he confessed his sinfulness. But his father isn't really concerned with his speech. He has already run out to meet his child, and he throws his arms around him and kisses him even before the boy makes his confession.

The new rite beautifully reflects Jesus' parable. It was formerly the penitent who began the encounter in confession—"Bless me, Father, for I have sinned" —very much as the prodigal son planned it. Now it is the confessor who takes the initiative, welcoming the penitent and creating an atmosphere of acceptance and love before there is any confession of sin. The new rite thus places a substantial burden on the confessor and on his ability to establish an atmosphere which many Catholics have not experienced in the confessional.

The change in atmosphere is capsulized in one remarkable sentence in the new rite: "Faithful Christians, as they experience and proclaim the mercy of God in their lives, celebrate with the priest the liturgy by which the Church continually renews itself" (#11). That sentence is a description of what confession is supposed to be. It suggests that we come to the sacrament because we have experienced the mercy of God and now want to proclaim it in a sacramental act. We have come in response to God's love, so that confession is actually a celebration. Is that what confession has been for most of us? The question reveals the kind of challenge the new rite poses.

Confession is also a celebration *with* the priest. In the courtroom model of confession, the priest was seen as one who stands somewhere *between* the penitent and God. In the new rite, the encounter with the confessor is horizontal rather than vertical. It is an encounter in faith and prayer rather than an encounter in the spirit of law and judgment. Contrast the dark confessional box with the practice of some of the churches in the East, where the ritual of confession is celebrated with confessor and penitent standing together before an icon. This is precisely the "horizontal" atmosphere fostered by the new rite.

The rite clarifies the priest's role in the process of reconciliation. The prayer of absolution completes or seals the change of heart which the penitent has manifested to the confessor. This prayer is the prayer of the Church, and the new rite carefully makes clear that it is not the priest who forgives sins. In fact, the priest is not even mentioned in the paragraph which talks about the meaning of absolution (#6). This is no accident. The authors of the rite were well aware of the many misunderstandings that have existed in the past regarding the priest's role.

The problem can be put in terms of the classic old statement: "Protestants go directly to God for forgiveness; Catholics go to a priest." The rite makes it clear that this is a false distinction. It is only the Lord who forgives sin; the priest declares that forgiveness in the name of the Lord and his Church. Throughout the rite, the confessor appears as a kind of "transparency," revealing and leading the penitent to see and proclaim the love of God. The ministry of the confessor is a ministry *within* and on behalf of the community of faith, not *over* it.

The sacramental moment of confession focuses on the love of God rather than on sin. The story of the prodigal son is again helpful. The boy's father does not moralize on the wrong he did. There is no discussion of the boy's sinfulness; his father does not even exhort him to avoid wrongdoing in the future. Jesus' parable contains a profound truth about the dynamic of forgiveness which we often overlook: There are many things that do not need to be analyzed or even verbalized in the act of forgiveness, once there has been a genuine affirmation of love.

The practice of confession has often been moralistic. By this I mean an *excessive preoccupation* with right and wrong, on the part of both priest and penitent. According to the new rite, confession is not primarily a time for the formation of conscience, moral instruction, or exhortations to sin no more. It is a liturgical act in which "the Church proclaims its faith and gives thanks to God for the freedom with which Christ has made us free" (#7).

There is a challenge here for both penitents and confessors, our attitudes, our reasons for going to confession. Confession is not a time for extensive counseling, or a forum for adult education. It is a time of celebration.

Confessors may have to rethink the approach they take in helping penitents to begin their confession.

The most spontaneous invitation has probably been along these lines: "Is there any problem you want to talk about, any major fault or sin that has been harming your relationship with God?"

This kind of invitation is valid enough, but I wonder if it really fits the spirit of the new rite. It is a moralistic invitation, because it focuses more on sin than on the mercy of God. Might it not be more appropriate for the confessor to begin by asking: "Do you really feel that God loves you, and that he has called you here because of his love for you?"

The first time I used that invitation I felt embarrassed. We Catholics are not used to evangelical-sounding language, perhaps least of all in confession. But the spirit of the new rite seems to call for that sort of approach, if the ritual itself is really to be a "celebration" in which Christians "experience and proclaim the mercy of God in their lives" (#11).

I have a beautiful painting of the oldest church building in our diocese. The painting was done by an Iowa artist from a photograph I had snapped while visiting the church one late December afternoon.

Fortunately I had my camera with me as I parked my car that cold winter day. Stepping out of the car I saw a scene I wanted to capture forever. The century-old building was silhouetted against the sun setting rapidly behind a grove of starkly nude trees. Grabbing my camera I shot several pictures. Well, I really hit the jackpot. The result is a beautiful painting hanging in my office.

One day a visitor looked at the painting and remarked, "Gosh Father, that's a beautiful frame, isn't it?" I nearly died. Frame my foot! Here was a fellow who missed the picture completely.

We do this all the time with our Catholic faith. We become so preoccupied with the framework of our religion that we miss the picture. When I recall how I have approached the sacrament of penance in the past, I can easily see why the sacrament has not been more fruitful in my own life.

I started early in life looking at the frame of the sacrament of penance. One Saturday afternoon when I was about nine I went to confession. The previous week had not been a particularly good one for me or anyone else around home and school. I had been a very bad boy!

I knelt down to prepare. Taking my prayer book with its list of sins, I proceeded to formulate my recitation. As I looked at the list, it seemed to me I had done all of them. When I got to the 6th and 9th commandments, I was puzzled. I didn't know what adultery was, nor did I know what coveting thy neighbor's wife meant.

"Oh well," I thought "I must have done them too, because I have really been bad lately."

The pastor was in the box and I began to recite my list a mile a minute. When I confessed that I had committed adultery, Father chuckled. "Do you know what adultery is?" he asked.

"No Father," I answered, "but if you've been as bad as me, you've probably done it too!"

OK, funny? A riot! But what a caricature of a beautiful sacrament. A little nine-year-old kid so preoccupied with laws, sins, externals—the framework—that he missed the beautiful picture he could have seen.

How different our confessions would be if we looked at the whole picture. The picture is that God loves us. If we'd prepare for confession by recalling all that God has done for us, how often he has shown his mercy, that he gave us the priceless gift of never-ending life, then we'd begin to see the staggering horror of our sins. We'd begin to see the ingratitude we display when we fail to respond to his never-ending offer of love. It's the experience of God's mercy and love, not laws and ritual which begin the process of conversion that ritual celebrates.

On one occasion I began to hear confessions during a communal celebration of the sacrament of reconciliation. I was in the sanctuary where I could get a view of the whole church. I noticed a crippled lady sitting in the front pew. There was a long line of penitents and it occurred to me that this poor woman would have to wait a long time. I motioned to the next penitent in line to wait and went down to the crippled lady to hear her confession. She thanked me and was able to leave shortly thereafter.

The next penitent began to cry after she had finished her confession. "Father, this has been the best confession I have ever made." I asked her why. "Well," she said, "when I saw you go to that crippled lady, I suddenly experienced a tremendous gratitude for all that God has done for me."

She continued: "That poor lady used more energy to walk from the church to her car than I need all day long. Not once have I ever thanked God for the good strong body he has given me."

Here was a lady who had gotten the picture. God's love had become real. It was there all the while, but suddenly, against the background of another's misfortune, her life was thrown into bold relief. She already had in abundance what the crippled woman would have rejoiced to have a small measure of. How good God had been to her and how little she had responded to his love! That memory changed her and she celebrated God's love without the framework of laws she had broken and a new ritual which heretofore had made her uncomfortable.

Sins are committed not because we break laws but because we damage or destroy relationships. You can't be reconciled with the law. Rituals do not celebrate laws, they celebrate relationships.

A real sense of sin presupposes that we have a strong sense of how much God loves us. One can't really feel sin, I think, unless one has felt love. According to the new rite, turning away from sin is a response to love. Conversion is a "profound change of the whole person by which one begins to consider, judge, and arrange one's life according to the holiness and love of God" (#6).

This suggests a whole new way of looking at sin. Sin is something that prevents me from seeing and arranging my life in response to God's love for me. This is much more than arranging one's life in accord with rule-keeping.

It is not just a moral sense of right and wrong that

should bring me to an awareness of my sinfulness, but above all a sense of God's love for me. And my confession of sinfulness, in a liturgical act, is most appropriately a response to the question, "Do I really believe the Lord loves me, no matter what wrong I have done?"

It is much easier to think of sin as the violation of a code than as a failure to arrange our lives in response to God's love. Rules and codes are simple. Dealing with a loving relationship is much more difficult. But it is quite tempting to seek absolution as a means of "feeling clean" again.

A friend of mine who directs retreats has adopted the practice of discouraging people from beginning their retreat with confession. He finds it more fitting for confession to be celebrated later in the retreat. This is very much in the spirit of the new rite and its definition of contrition. Coming to judge one's life in response to the love of God instead of rule-keeping takes some time and reflection. And the new rite invites us to seek absolution for more profound reasons than "feeling clean" or "setting the record straight."

This presupposes that there is something going on inside us, something special to proclaim and celebrate. The new rite locates confession within the Church's larger ministry of reconciliation, which begins in baptism and which continues in every celebration of the eucharist. The eucharist is our normal and ordinary sacrament of reconciliation, because it celebrates the "sacrifice which has made our peace with God" (#2).

So confession is clearly a special sacrament, something for special occasions, the fruit of a special experience. "How often should I go to confession?" One can no longer give a set answer to that question. The definition of contrition given in the new rite implies that we come to the sacrament with a strong sense of a new beginning.

We used to preach the benefits of confession in this way: "Go to confession often. It's good for you, it is an occasion of grace."

The new rite suggests that we have been putting the cart before the horse. The thrust of the new rite is this: "Respond to the grace of a new beginning. Then go to confession and celebrate that new beginning."

The rite calls for a whole new style of preaching. In the past we have preached a discipline much more than a sacrament. In the discipline approach, confession comes out as one of the good and graced things Catholics should do. But in an authentic sacramental approach, which is the approach of the new rite, we have to give serious attention to the experience which we bring to the sacrament.

Sacramental confession is a peak moment in a total process of conversion. A change of heart is the most important act of the penitent. Apart from this inner change of attitude, this sense of a new beginning, confession and absolution have no meaning and no effect.

We do not go to confession to "get" forgiveness. We go there to celebrate it. The experience of grace is already there, the love of God is already there. Confession is not itself the new beginning. The new beginning has begun before we come to the sacrament, and before absolution is given. Sacramental confession celebrates something that has already begun.

The new rite does not deal with the question of confession for children, but it does contain some principles that challenge our present practices. The rite clearly calls for a high degree of self-awareness, and it will force us to continue thinking about the appropriate age for a child's first experience of *individual confession*. As many catechists and pastors have urged, communal liturgies for children are often a far more effective introduction to the sacrament than individual confession.

If a child has no real sense of a new beginning, no sense of a "profound change by which one begins to arrange one's life in accord with the love of God," what can the sacrament possibly mean? If "the most important act of the penitent is contrition" (#6), and if a child has not reached the sense of contrition which the rite calls for, we should certainly call into question the wisdom of trotting eight-year-olds over to the church for confession on the Thursdays before First Fridays.

Confession is not a sacrament of initiation into the Christian life. The sacraments of initiation are baptism, confirmation, and eucharist. The new rite of confession makes it extremely clear that confession is not meant to be a training ground for a good Catholic life. Confession is a special celebration of God's love for us, and it presupposes a genuine experience of sinfulness, which is much more than rule-breaking.

Perhaps parents ought to experience the new rite of confession themselves, and reflect thoroughly on that experience, before they come to any decision about the right age for the first individual confession of their children.

Some ten years ago, two of my nephews were scuffling in the living room of their home. One of the boys accidentally struck a table, tumbling a beautiful vase to the floor. The vase was completely smashed. It had a special significance to their mother, my sister. It was a gift from her neighbors at the time of my mother's death two years before. Of all her possessions, this vase was most prized by my sister because it symbolized a link to our mother's memory as well as a sign of a neighborhood's affection.

When my sister Mary heard the crash, she came flying from the kitchen only to see this cherished vase smashed to pieces. She broke down and cried. Two repentant boys stood helpless before the scattered array of ceramic debris. Finally thirteen-year-old Michael spoke: "Mom, I'll put it together again." Through her tears Mary responded impatiently, "Don't be silly. Just sweep up that mess." With that she left the room.

Michael was undaunted. Carefully he picked up every piece and sliver, put the pieces into a sack, and took them to his room.

Seven years went by. In June, 1976, Mary suffered a massive heart attack. Three of her nine children living in other states were hastily called home. Michael came from Washington State.

During the ten days he was home, Michael spent most of his time alone in his former room. This did not appear unusual to the family because he had always spent a lot of time there, studying, reading, and writing.

Near the end of the ten days, he came downstairs one afternoon grinning from ear to ear. In his hands Michael held the perfectly restored vase he had broken to pieces seven years before. The family gasped. They were stunned. Michael had spent nearly ten days patiently restoring, piece by piece, sliver by sliver, a vase which once meant so much to his mother.

Michael asked his family to keep the vase a secret. He bade his mother goodbye at the hospital and returned to Washington.

Two weeks later, Mary returned home. The first thing she spotted was the restored vase. She cried, not so much because the vase had been restored, but because it symbolized and celebrated a love Michael undoubtedly imagined had been tarnished and damaged throughout the years. The restored vase was Michael's unspoken word of repentance, love, and reconciliation. The restored vase was his sacrament of reconciliation with his mother even though she had long forgotten the incident.

My sister told me that in all of her suffering she kept that restored vase in her damaged heart. It was, as she said, a continuous act of loving reaching out to her saying, "If the love of a boy for his mother can mend an impossibly broken vase, the love of God and the care of doctors and nurses can mend a broken heart."

Sinfulness smashes the "vase" of our lives. Repentance is the gnawing hunger and thirst to restore and reconcile the beauty God has created. Sacrament is the celebration of renewed oneness. The sacrament of reconciliation is a renewal of baptism, our beginning of beginnings. Out of our sinfulness arises a new appreciation and consciousness of God's love graciously gifted to us in Jesus and gradually unfolded by God's holy spirit.

Repentance is what *we* do; reconciliation is what *God* does. Sacrament is what *God and people do* to celebrate both.

Pastorally speaking, I would have to admit that much of the non-acceptance of the new rite of penance has to do with misunderstanding of the theology upon which the new rite has been constructed. When the new rite uses words like "penance" and "reconciliation," they are heard against a background of understanding and experience of the former rite. Words are not isolated from the understanding and experiences which prompt them to be written or spoken. When words fall on deaf ears, usually it's because the hearers have not shared the background out of which the words come.

This is not a new problem. It has always been the Achilles heel of genuine communication. A word is only effective to the extent that our understanding and experience approximate the understanding and experience of the speaker. If there is little equity of understanding between speaker and hearer, writer and reader, the most that can be expected is information—when formation and transformation have been intended.

A good example of this is the use of the word "celebrate." How do American Catholics, understanding one meaning of the word celebrate, understand this sentence from the rite, which we have already quoted several times? "Faithful Christians, as they experience and proclaim the mercy of God in their lives, celebrate with the priest the liturgy by which the Church continually renews itself." What does the new rite intend by the word "celebrate"? What does the average Catholic understand by that word? Does our previous experience of confession approximate the kind of celebration with which we are familiar? Does the new rite envision another understanding of celebration?

My past experience of confession has hardly been a celebration. Accustomed to the dark and forbidding confessional box, encountering a priest whose role seemed to be more that of judge than proclaimer of mercy, and relieved that I had satisfied the demands of my duly imposed penance, celebration in the sacramental sense has been difficult to equate with my past experiences of celebration. Give me the celebration of a last-minute winning Notre Dame touchdown any old day.

But wait a minute! Can there be celebration apart from bells, balloons and booze? Have we confused the trappings of celebration with the meaning of celebration? Let's look more closely at the word.

"Celebrate" comes from the latin *celeber,* meaning

"a much frequented place." The *celeber* was a pagan temple where people gathered to placate, praise, thank, and petition their gods. What they did, said, and sang in these places came to be known as "celebrations." Originally these "celebrations" were prayers, hymns and gestures, of people to their gods. We call it liturgy.

We are the "much frequented places" God dwells within.

We are "the temples of the Holy Spirit," as St. Paul puts it. When we "celebrate" the sacrament of reconciliation we acknowledge God's place in our hearts. Though the prodigal son left his father, the father never left his son. His son was always in his heart. The son's return prompted the father to exclaim, "We are going to have a celebration!"

True repentance is a liberation, not a put-down. God cannot re-occupy hearts halfway. It's as the old song says, "All or nothing at all." We miss the good news of repentance when we imagine an enraged and furious God almost grudgingly receiving us poor sinners back into his favor. Such was the mistake of the younger son. He showed poor judgment when he left his father and repeated the mistake when he decided to return as a servant. "I no longer deserve to be called your son; treat me as one of your paid servants."

What the Gospel leaves unsaid often impresses me as much as what it does say. When the prodigal son blurted out his carefully rehearsed speech, his father paid absolutely no attention to him. One can imagine the hurt the father felt when his son so grossly underrated his forgiveness. Without as much as the slightest hint that this servant status might be an appropriate "satisfaction," the father called to the servants to prepare a feast. Very often true repentance is ruined because, as someone once wrote, "Your God is too small." When our image of God is so small that we imagine only a partial reconciliation, there really isn't very much to celebrate, is there?

The prodigal son's mentality is a frustrating obstacle for confessors. It is incredible that so many penitents feel that they must "make up to God" before they are satisfied that God has fully forgiven them. It's the old problem of courtroom justice where you "get" according as you "earn." Many penitents treat themselves as the elder son wanted the father to treat his repentant brother. Shouldn't his younger brother earn the father's favor just as he had done all these years?

The new rite of penance, of itself, will never change the masochistic mentality demanding that God beat the hell out of us before he pours the grace of heaven into us. Without a change of mentality, the new rite will be just another case of pouring new wine into old wine skins. The rite in fact calls for a whole new way of looking at the picture.

Chapter 8

A PASTOR'S EXPERIENCE

My mother was a great storyteller. One story about her grandfather was always good for a bundle of laughs. A prosperous neighbor had just purchased a spanking new Maxwell automobile. Eager to show off his ultimate sign of affluence, he drove over to my mother's home one Sunday afternoon.

The family had just finished dinner when the "gas buggy" swung through the barnyard gate. The entire family, seven children, parents, and, of course, Grandpa, made a bee-line to the barnyard. Not one of them had ever seen an automobile "in the flesh."

After much oohing and aahing, kicking of tires, and the elbow-rubbing of shiny brass headlights, the neighbor invited Grandpa to sit at the wheel. Cautiously, the old gentleman settled himself in the driver's seat. But he wasn't all that comfortable and kept moving his legs in various directions. Finally, he looked at the neighbor and snorted, "Where's the stirrups in this damn thing?"

Sometimes I think many penitents are trying to

find the stirrups in the new rite of reconciliation. I see this story as a good analogy because the revised rite of the sacrament of penance represents much more than a change in externals. It is not merely a new way of going to confession, any more than the automobile represented a new way of riding a hayless horse. The automobile signaled the beginning of a radically new way of living, so all-embracing that every aspect of daily living has been changed. So far as I can see, the new rite of penance envisions a complete rethinking of our Catholic faith, embracing every aspect of that faith.

As a pastor, I can testify that for the most part Catholics are uncomfortable with the new rite. Our discomfort, however, is not due to reconciliation rooms, confessing face to face, or the various steps which make up the new rite. In time we'll get used to all of this. No, our distress lies much deeper and is, it seems to me, the real reason why people are remaining away from confession in droves. What the new rite is demanding is what Jesus demanded—repentance. This calls for a far more radical change than exchanging confessional boxes for reconciliation rooms, or going to confession face to face. Let's not kid ourselves about this any longer. The message is getting through and we Catholics know it. We know that the Church is no longer fooling around with new patches on old cloth, and that's why we're squirming.

Sacraments are signs which indicate a reality. If the reality is not present, then sacraments become little more than memorabilia of a bygone age, good perhaps for nostalgia but hardly effective. Signs are useless unless they signify something real, valuable, authentic, and timely. I remember approaching a railroad-crossing sign on a country road. The sign said something to me—slow down! I looked to see if a train were approaching. Seeing none, I passed the sign and was surprised to discover that the tracks had been removed.

I chuckled at the thought that here was a sign which signified nothing, except to recall that trains once ran here. I have been over that road many times since. I no longer "stop, look, or listen," or even slow down. In fact, I don't even look at the sign anymore because I know there is no reason to stop, look, and listen. The sign is useless because the tracks are not there.

I am not suggesting by this analogy that we have lost our faith and that the new rite will restore it. Quite the contrary. The new rite offers a new understanding for a faith always in need of renewal. When we lined up for Saturday confessions in our parish churches, we expressed an authentic faith based upon a particular understanding of that faith. It is arrogant to imply that all of that was wrong, valueless, or unnourishing. There was a tremendous display of faith in our particular understanding of God, Church, grace, sin and sacraments as we went about the practice of that faith.

There is, on the other hand, something quite arrogant about the supposition that this understanding of faith is the only understanding. "We've never done it that way before" are the seven last words which always place religion somewhere between nostalgia and superstition. If there are no further understandings of faith, then religion either becomes Pavlovian conditioning so that its signs and expressions cause no more than nostalgic salivation; or it becomes a way of manipulating a God whom we force to stop, look and listen to us.

As I write, it has been well over a year since the new rite of penance was put into effect. Previous revisions of the sacraments taught me not to expect great success. I can still remember starry-eyed idealists who fifteen years ago were predicting packed churches when all of those millions of vernacular-hungry people could at last worship in their own language. The irony of it all is that the churches were packed when the predictions were made, and they aren't now.

Penitents are not lined up before the reconciliation rooms, any more than they were before the confessional boxes on the eve of the new rite. Those who do come to confession with some regularity make up two quite distinct categories.

By far the greater number come with the old grocery-list mentality. And yet, something new is beginning to happen to them. The new rite, I believe, is laying bare for them the poverty of the old rite. I find many of them now saying, "I really don't know what's sinful and what isn't." Another complaint is "I'm confessing the same sins everytime I go to confession. There must be something deeper inside of me I'm not getting at." One teenager put it this picturesque way in a classroom discussion: "Father, going to confession is like cutting the grass—you feel good when you finish but you know darn well it's going to grow again." Some penitents of this category get right to the point: "What in the heck is this new rite getting at?"

As far as I'm concerned, questions and comments like these are healthy signs. The problem is, you can't turn reconciliation rooms into adult education classrooms. If the new rite of penance has done anything, it has exposed the need for a massive catechesis and an evangelization process among both teenagers and adult Catholics. Those who go to confession with any regularity may be just beginning to see this. Is it no more than coincidence that the last two Roman Synods have dealt with evangelization and catechesis? I think not.

Without an on-going adult catechesis, and without good solid theological reflection on Christ's message of repentance and reconciliation, these first stirrings of faith within the hearts of "grocery list" penitents will be stillborn. The new rite of penance is not predicated on the Baltimore Cathechism, but the faith of millions of Catholics is. These two ships are going to pass silently in the night unless evangelization and catechesis becomes a way of life for millions of Catholics. Without it, the new rite of penance can have little meaning even for those who are beginning to see light in its wisdom.

The second category of penitents, not nearly as large as the first, have confirmed for me the remarks I made above. These are people who for the past two or three years have participated regularly in adult education programs. Their confessions have a marked quality revealing that they are "hitting the mark." In general, this is how this group of people differs from the "grocery list" crowd.

1. Rather than listing sins, they talk about relationships. If, for example, a mother confesses impatience, she is careful to note some obstacle within herself that does damage to the relationships she ought to enjoy with her children. How curious the number of times parents make comments like this: "I quit getting angry at my daughter when I discovered that she was a perfect mirror of my own attitudes and habits." Or, "It just hit me one day, God created my children in his image and likeness, and I blow my top when they don't turn out to be my image and likeness."

Couples who have made marriage encounters resonate to the new rite of penance. Once they understand that successful marriages flow out of deepening marital relationships, they find the new rite of penance a kind of follow-up to their newly found discovery as well as a celebration of the progress they are making.

I also see in penitents of this category an awakening consciousness of renewed relationships with God. Some penitents admit that in the past they rarely thought of God when preparing for confession. What was important to them were the laws they had broken.

A few penitents indicate a renewed relationship with themselves. "If God loves me, surely I can learn to love myself." Or, "If I can't forgive myself, I'll never be able to forgive others." Remarks like these clearly show that people are learning to deal with their hurts, their wounds, and their scars. They know that before they can have healthy relationships with others, they must have healthy relationships with themselves.

2. Today's penitents have a greater awareness of community. Again, they are picking this up from cursillos, marriage encounters, and adult education opportunities they have responded to. As a result, they are conscious of the social implications of their own sinfulness. They understand reconciliation in a broader perspective than "I ain't mad at nobody." All sinfulness is madness because its ego-centricity weakens or destroys the very sacramentality of the Church. Reconciliation becomes much more than an apology for a cross word, a momentary impatience, or a tasteless insult. Penitents with a good grasp of community understand reconciliation as a way of living, an on-going process of carrying out God's "hidden plan": that he "bring together under Christ, as head, everything in the heavens and everything on earth" (Ephesians 1: 9–10).

What I have noticed most about community-conscious penitents is that their confessions are like "progress reports." They speak of improving relationships at home, at work, or in the parish. Words like "atmosphere," "climate," and "environment" are used to indicate progress in community-building. I am astonished at the number of children and teenagers who recognize their own role in creating an atmosphere conducive to healthy community life. They admit that their own selfishness is largely responsible for an atmosphere of hostility and open warfare in their homes. Frequently youngsters report, "Things are better at home because I know home is all of us, not just me."

In our parish school, the American bishops' document on education, *To Teach as Jesus Did,* is a kind of constitutional charter. Its emphasis on message, community, and service is little by little having an impact on the children. This is showing up in their confessions. Very often they confess only one sin. But then they show the implications of what that act of sinfulness has done to those around them. Sometimes I can hardly believe the quality of their confessions and the almost intuitive grasp they have of the new rite and the attitudes the new rite invites them to change. With their community-consciousness, many youngsters have a much better idea of reconciliation than adults.

3. Penitents of the second category focus their confession on God's love rather than laws. They are not so much concerned with sin as with the mercy of God. They clearly reflect a familiarity with the scriptures and reveal that their prayer life flows from them. They see their sinfulness against a background of ways Jesus treated sinners, and they are inspired with the hope that God shows the same mercy to them. Sins are no longer regarded as violations of laws but as failures to respond to God's love.

This consciousness of God's love and mercy is what I touch on most in dealing with the grocery-list penitents. Very little is to be gained, given the massiveness of the catechetical task yet to be done, in throwing up my hands in despair and retreating to the five Our Fathers and Hail Marys syndrome. I use scripture to good advantage, letting the power of God's word work in ways I little realize. I find that the use of God's word relaxes penitents enough so that they are able to touch sinful attitudes. They see themselves, for example, as the prodigal son, Zacchaeus, Mary Magdalene, or the good thief. It dawns on them, sometimes in a genuine evangelizing moment, that if Jesus loved these sinners so generously, he also loves them just as generously.

4. Confessions of enlightened penitents are marked by prayerfulness. Generally their prayer is that of thanksgiving and praise. Frequently they pray spontaneously and invite me to pray over them. Again, the penitents bring to confession a rich experience of prayer they have found in prayer groups, charismatic prayer meetings, and cursillo group reunions. Where this experience is lacking, the confessor cannot expect much more than the routine act of contrition or at best a reading of one of the prayers suggested in the new rite.

Here is where the confessor can help create a more prayerful atmosphere. After the recitation of the act of contrition, I usually pray for the penitent. If I know the penitent's name, I include his or her name in the prayer in order to make it as personal and special as possible. Confession is liturgy and therefore the whole action ought to be a prayerful experience. Penitents appreciate the confessor's prayerfulness and rarely fail to respond to it. Usually, the confessor can touch on some sinful attitude suggested by the penitent's sins, make a reference to God's special love for sinners, and appeal to the penitent's desire for the peace and joy which springs from deepened relationships with God and with neighbor.

5. A banner I once saw suggests a quality I observe in the second category of penitents: "God isn't finished with me yet." These penitents see confession as an on-going process, a kind of lifetime passover from sinfulness to life in Christ. They are under no illusion that any one celebration of the sacrament of penance is the "I found it" magic wand that once and for all removes sinfulness.

This attitude and approach to the sacrament of penance is quite consistent with other experiences in our lives. Regardless of how important any relationship is, if it is to last, there must be follow-up. Friendships need renewal. In-service training is essential if skill and expertise are to be maintained. Even periodic checkups with the doctor are essential if one expects bodily and mental health. The Christian life is a journey and we are pilgrims making that journey. The sacrament of penance, like the eucharist, never loses sight that in baptism we died to sinfulness and rose with Christ. Confession is baptism's on-going renewal.

When it came time to choose a location for a reconciliation room in our parish church, I found the baptistry most appropriate. While hearing confessions there, I find it helpful to draw the penitent's attention to the room's former status. I use a "roots" theme reminding them that the sacrament of penance is renewed faithfulness to baptismal commitment. By taking the time to confess their sinfulness, they show that they care about that commitment, are responding to God's love, and are celebrating their life in Christ. The baptismal "roots" theme is especially effective for parishioners who were baptized there. It's like a homecoming.

As confessor I am not a shriver, the *American Heritage Dictionary* to the contrary. The sacrament of penance is a liturgical act, and in it the confessor presides. It is unfortunate that the word "preside" carries a rather pompous connotation in its American usage. I suppose that's because too many people in authority preside pompously. The Latin, *praesidere,* means to "sit in front of." A little more research, however, enabled me to discover that presiders also settle and calm those who come to them.

The president of any liturgical act, especially the sacrament of penance, sets a tone and creates an atmosphere which is both settling and calming. If the sacrament of penance is par excellence a sacrament of peace, the president of that action must be above all a man of peace. The peaceful, calming, and settling manner of the confessor will be remembered far longer than any other aspect of the penitent's confession.

Whenever I think of the ideal confessor, the ideal presider, I think of Fr. Billy Coughlin, pastor of Holy Family Parish, Council Bluffs, Iowa. He died shortly before Vatican II. Confessor to many priests in the vicinity, he was the kindest, gentlest, and most "calming and settling" man I had ever met. Hearing confessions was a "natural" for him. As confessor he was who he was, no more, no less. He knew how to welcome, how to make you feel at home, and how to say goodbye. If ever a priest gave me a "feel" for God it was Fr. Billy Coughlin.

Fr. Coughlin's ability to integrate who he was with what he did taught me more about liturgical presiding than any book, workshop, or seminar on the subject. When I preside at a sacramental action, I try to be who I am. God is not to be found only in the rubrics, gestures, and the words of the liturgical action. He is in the persons who use the rubrics, the gestures, and the words of the liturgy to celebrate the gift of God's loving presence. Whenever a priest brings all that he really is—his qualities, traits, virtues, even his limitations—to liturgy, he enables the Holy Spirit to do God's work—reconciliation, and the fruits of reconciliation, peace and joy.

Twenty-five years ago I was confessing face-to-face to Fr. Coughlin. I lament the fact that his parishioners did not have that opportunity. I am sure though that even in the confessional box Fr. Coughlin communicated to the parishioners much of his warmth and gentleness. How blest would those parishioners be today to experience the sacramental presence of his wholeness and his holiness.

To preside means to employ the fulness of who you are. Presiding is not role-playing. When a confessor assumes a role he imagines the sacrament of penance calls for, he does violence to the sacrament. As a result, sacramental celebrations come off as unreal, not related to life, and altogether staged.

When a person walks into the reconciliation room

I welcome that person not according to some formula I have memorized, but by a greeting appropriate to the kind of person I am. I am by nature an enthusiastic person. I like people and am delighted when people visit me. If I am to be faithful to both myself and the sacrament, I want that enthusiasm and delight to be experienced in the reconciliation room. I want people to feel at home wherever I am, including the reconciliation room.

I always call the person by name if I know him or her, unless the person has chosen to confess behind the screen. I presume anonymity is one of the reasons people choose the screen. In our parish most of the parishioners confess face to face. This is the manner I am addressing myself to here. If I do not know the penitent by name, I ask for it. Very often I use this pre-confession stage, this "calming down" period to thank parishioners for some work they are doing for the community. Lectors, ministers of communion, parish council and board of education members, members of parish societies, bingo workers (yes, our parish has the eighth sacrament), CCD teachers and lay ministers who regularly visit the sick: these are some of the people I thank. What I am doing here, I think, is integrating their lives into the action of the sacrament. Sacraments celebrate life. I want people to realize that much of their lives is a response to God's grace and invite them to see for themselves that their sinfulness is unfaithfulness to God's grace.

After the sign of the cross, I read a short passage of scripture. I read the passage slowly and calmly, emphasizing certain words and phrases. I cannot over-estimate the effectiveness of God's word in the celebration of this sacrament. Even though it is optional, it is well worth the extra time it takes. In several instances I discover that penitents make reference to the passage while confessing their sins.

After a brief reflection on the scripture passage, I invite the penitents to confess their sins and where possible to surface false attitudes which they feel may have caused these sins. Quite frankly, there are penitents who do not understand what I mean. In those cases I simply let the matter drop and invite them to tell their sins. More instruction is needed, and, as I have said, the reconciliation room is not the place for adult education.

I am always conscious of the prayerfulness that ought to prevail throughout each confession. Frequently I offer a short prayer for the penitent and invite him or her to pray. Usually I can expect the act of contrition. A surprising number of penitents pray spontaneously. These prayers are brief, filled with thanksgiving, and always heartfelt.

The assignment of penances is diversified. Sometimes I invite the penitent to spend a few moments in prayer before leaving the church. If they have confessed, for example, ill-will towards others, I ask penitents to pray for those who may have inflicted injury upon them. If sins confessed include quarreling in the home, I invite the penitent to make amends, to be reconciled, and to restore peace. I emphasize that the priest's absolution is not a magic wand, but rather a celebration of a conversion motivating the penitent to restore a damaged relationship.

A penance ought not to carry with it a note of finality. Rather it is like a baton in a relay race. The penance ought to say in effect, "My confession is not ended," or as the song says, "We've only just begun." Penance means renewal and that process never ends. I ask penitents to see themselves as sacraments of penance. They are a "priestly people" engaged daily in the reconciling work of the Lord. They too are the "stewards of the manifold grace of God," ministering reconciliation and healing in their homes and community. If confessors can enable penitents to appreciate and practice their priestliness, the whole world can become a reconciliation room.

When I began the new rite of penance in our parish, I delayed the rite of laying on of hands. I continued the practice of raising my right arm as confessors were accustomed to do in the confessional box. People were already very nervous with the other changes, and I felt this gesture needed to be delayed so that more catechesis could be given.

The custom of laying on hands is ancient although somewhat foreign to our culture. One commentator makes this point: "In Jewish practice the laying on of hands was very common. When hands were laid on, there was held to be a transference of certain qualities from one person to another . . . the dominating factor was the character of the man who laid on the hands."[14]

This explains why people pressed close to Jesus, even touching his garments. The apostles continued the practice of laying on hands especially when they heard that people had accepted God's word (Acts

8:14). They were convinced that God's spirit filled them, and they were eager to impart the Holy Spirit to others.

The Catholic experience of the laying on of hands had been confined to the sacraments of confirmation and holy orders prior to Vatican II. Since that time, however, it has been incorporated into the revisions of the sacrament of the sick and the sacrament of reconciliation. I decided that the catechesis for a penitential laying on of hands should include not only verbal instruction but a non-sacramental use of the practice. I invited parents to bring their little children to communion with them so that I could lay hands on the children. The suggestion met with instant success.

Another practice of the gesture is to bless the members of households just before I leave. After the blessing I place my hands on each person's head, sometimes silently, sometimes with a very short prayer. If I forget, I am gently reminded by one of the family. Finally, in all cases whenever I visit the sick, I make it a practice to impose my hands with an accompanying short prayer.

With this kind of catechesis, the imposition of hands became "a natural" for the sacrament of penance. There is none of the awkwardness or artificiality that may have accompanied the gesture had I begun with it. In many ways, the varied use of this ancient practice in our parish has brought me closer to the parishioners. There is a kind of presence within the parish I have never experienced before in any parish. Once again the Church has shown wisdom in reviving a part of her heritage. The "newness" is delightful.

How you say goodbye is as important as how you say welcome. When a penitent prepares to leave, I always stand and shake hands, offering him or her the peace of Christ. Usually I accompany the elderly to the door, asking them to pray for me and the parish or to say hello to members of the family. I assure them that I enjoyed the visit and with a grin say, "Let's get together again—soon."

There are hazards in being a "settling, calming" confessor. Some penitents get so relaxed that their confessions become revelations of all their problems, physical, mental, financial, and family. As confessor I do not see myself as a counselor. A confessor recalls God's love and mercy, helps the penitents celebrate that saving truth, and proclaims God's forgiveness. When penitents get into the voluminous details of their lives, I tactfully remind them that other penitents are awaiting their turn and I suggest a visit at the rectory. This must be done kindly, gently, and with care. But it must be done.

I welcome the emphasis given to the ways priests preside. Good presidential action is essential to good liturgy. At the very least it is good manners; at the very most it is wholeness, and that's the doorway to holiness.

After thirty years I find that I am only a neophyte at the art of presiding. I am much more a neophyte as a penitent. But the more I become acclimated to the spirit of the new rite as a penitent, the better a confessor I become. For me as penitent, the secret of the new rite is preparation for confession. The three preparatory steps suggested by the rite, prayer for light, scripture, and examination of conscience, have proven very beneficial.

The prayer for light is not necessarily the recitation of prayers. It is simply a few minutes of calm, of recalling God's loving and healing presence, a few minutes of stillness. Why do we always feel we must do the talking? Wherever there is silence, there is a good chance of finding God. Quiet, silence, and stillness are the best atmosphere we can create for hearing God's invitations.

My scripture preparation is usually a random selection of texts. Sometimes I wonder what in the world a particular scripture passage which I have randomly selected has to do with the sacrament of penance. Almost always, however, such passages provide amazing insights and turn out to be the very graced light I prayed for.

On one occasion my random selection turned out to be the story of the two disciples on the way to Emmaus (Luke 24). I was tempted to go for another selection. I stuck to Emmaus and was treated to an insight. The words, "Our own hope had been that he would be the one to set Israel free" caught my eye. I saw myself in those two disciples. They did not recognize Jesus because they were so preoccupied with the messiah of *their* hopes. The messiah of their hopes died on the cross. Their hopes could carry them no further. I asked myself, "Have I too missed Jesus Christ in my midst because I have limited him to my hopes?" I began to understand that the failure of my own hopes was but the beginning of genuine hope in Jesus Christ. I saw that the dying of my own hopes was but an integral part of the paschal mystery leading me to a new recognition of Jesus Christ. My confession that day became a real celebration because from an unexpected source God revealed himself to me in a most surprising yet "right-on-the-mark" way.

As I begin my confession I like to thank God for specific ways he has shown his love. If I can experience God's love for me I can easily experience the hideousness of my sinfulness. True to my current understanding of the new rite, I'm interested in getting at the disease. Sometimes this is difficult, and I deeply appreciate any help my confessor provides. He never fails to point out some good quality he notes in me, with a suggestion that my current behavior is really an unfaithfulness to myself, to the real person God created me to be. This approach has not only been beneficial to me, I have tried it with other penitents.

I am glad that I have to struggle with the revised rite of penance as penitent, because it has given me a genuine sympathy for my penitents. I hope they can see that in me. When we struggle together we can be sure we are building community. I do not wish to demean our strengths, but I believe God does his work best in our weaknesses and in our poverty. God's work is reconciliation. For me the sacrament of reconciliation, as confessor and penitent, has been my Achilles' heel. It is the Achilles' heel of parish life today. But if I really believe that the poor in spirit are blessed, I must also believe that this sacrament will become a shining strength in the building of the Christian community.

Chapter 9

BEYOND CONFESSION

If the Lord's forgiveness is always there for us, why bother with confession? If confession doesn't "give" forgiveness, why bother "getting absolved"?

Questions like these are very common today. They point up how difficult it is to develop the attitude that confession, like any other sacrament, is *celebration*. Absolution, more than any other sacramental sign, has been legalistically rather than sacramentally understood. This chapter will take up forms of sacramental reconciliation other than confession. We will especially look at general absolution and communal celebrations of penance. But unless we can overcome the legalism associated with absolution, the same legalism will plague our understanding of general absolution.

So let us begin by asking: Why absolution? Why absolution in *any* form, individual or communal?

The word "absolution" itself is a stumbling block, because it is a legalistic word. Let me suggest another term, a sacramental one. Absolution is a sacramental sign-action, it is a *proclamation of God's word of forgiveness.*

Sin is not a private thing between me and God. Sin affects other people, and not simply in those instances where others are directly harmed by what we do. Long before our sinfulness actually touches other people, it affects our attitudes toward them and relations with them. So, ultimately, there really is no such thing as purely "private" sin. This is why the process of penance finally engages the Church. It is why, right from the beginning of our history, the Church has come up with different forms of proclaiming God's forgiveness.

In fact, the proclamation of God's word of forgiveness has to do with the whole reason why there *is* a Church. A sacramental sign of reconciliation is not going to tell a person just how to cope with his or her past. This is the work of a counselor or a psychologist. Although ministers have functioned in that role, often very effectively, the role of counselor should be very clearly distinguished from the ministerial role of announcing forgiveness and reconciliation with the community.

The purpose of the sacramental sign is distinct from that of therapeutic counseling. Or rather, *the sacramental sign has a therapeutic function of its own.* Its purpose is to tell the penitent—in words, in the laying on of hands, in a handshake of reconciliation, in the breaking of the bread—that she has a future, that he does not have to go through life looking back at the wrong he has done, that she can move into the future at peace and with confidence that the past no longer matters. The Church exists precisely to proclaim this freeing word of God, this freeing from the bonds of guilt. All of the most basic ritual actions of the Church are centered around this kind of proclamation.

What form should the sign of reconciliation take? Historically it has taken many forms, of which absolution in the confessional is only one. Beyond baptism itself and the new beginning which that sacrament signifies, *the most traditional sacrament of reconciliation is clearly the eucharist.* Any eucharistic liturgy is a call to enter more deeply into the process of conversion-reconciliation. The word of God invites us to undergo a constant change of heart, to come to terms with ourselves and with what the Spirit of God is calling us to become. The liturgy of the word calls us to the work of reconciliation; and the sharing of the eucharistic meal is itself an expression of reconciliation at work.

This is what is meant by calling the Mass a "sacrifice." Borrowing an image from the ancient practice of blood rituals, the Christian tradition very early began referring to the eucharist as a "sacrificial" meal. Like the old sacrifices which were understood to reconcile us with God, this meal proclaims the reconciling death of Jesus. Our action with bread and wine announces "God in Christ reconciling the world to himself, not holding people's faults against them" (2 Cor 6:19). The signs of bread and wine proclaim our unity with him who died in order to draw together the scattered children of God; and they proclaim our dedication to the work of making a unity among people. Thus the greeting of peace, a very essential part of the communion rite, expresses our willingness to reconcile ourselves with our brothers and sisters, to break down the barriers that exist between people and so to find reconciliation with God.

The eucharist therefore is and always has been the *normal and ordinary* Christian sacrament of reconciliation. This is a fact that came to be overlooked or forgotten, owing especially to the medieval analysis of the sacraments, which dealt with the forgiveness of sin under the small headings of baptism or confession, and not in the larger context of the Church as community of reconciliation, celebrating its basic identity in the eucharist.

The Council of Trent had practical pastoral reasons, in its time, for insisting that a person guilty of mortal sin should confess before receiving communion. This was a disciplinary measure. It did not change the theological fact that *formal confession only makes explicit a reconciliation that is already present in the eucharistic action.* This is not a new truth. One theologian affirmed this subordination of confession to the efficacy of the eucharist in the full assembly of Trent. Then as now, confession "serves only to stress clearly a structural component of the eucharist within the total mystery of Christian reconciliation."[15]

An adequate understanding of the eucharist itself is at stake here. I would urge that, for all the liturgical renewal we have accomplished, not nearly enough has been said or preached about the eucharist as sign of reconciliation. A good many Catholics in recent years have sensed what many of their pastors, threatened by the decline of individual confession, have not yet grasped: that to abandon confession as a regular religious practice is not at all to abandon the sacrament of reconciliation. This *sensus communis fidelium,* this good sense of the faithful needs to be picked up, built upon, brought through preaching to a level of conscious awareness. To do so is only to take seriously what we have always meant by calling the eucharist a sacrifice.

The ritual of the eucharist and the rubrics of the *Ordo missae* must also be taken seriously. The eucharist will not become apparent as the primary Christian sacrament of reconciliation so long as the ritual action emphasizes private communion with God. The primary symbolism of the mass consists in a communal breaking of the bread, a communal sharing of the cup. We simply must get beyond the excuses we make for eliminating the sharing of the cup (most of which are not supported by the *Ordo missae*), or for reducing the breaking of the bread to a barely noticeable splitting of a white wafer. It is all very well for theology to speak of the presence of the Lord whole and entire under the species of each particle of bread. This theological principle prescinds entirely from the far more basic question of how we are to celebrate the eucharist as Jesus intended it. We have a long way to go in realizing the eucharist as an *experience* of reconciliation, a ritual experience which *speaks* reconciliation.

In addition to the eucharist, the normal and ordinary sacrament of reconciliation, there has also been throughout Christian history a "special" sacramental sign, which has taken various forms. It involves some kind of oral confession in which Christians verbalize, privately or in a communal setting, their need for forgiveness. They then hear proclaimed the good news of God's forgiveness which belongs to them by reason of their interior conversion. Their situation is that of people who approached Jesus and heard from him the words, "Your sins are forgiven; go in peace."

The need for this special sign of reconciliation will always exist—and indeed in a form like that of individual confession. If Catholics today are reacting against a misuse or over-use of confession, many Protestants are rediscovering the value of this ritual which entirely disappeared from many Protestant traditions. Benjamin Garrison, a Methodist pastor, tells the following story which exemplifies far better than any theological principle the need for a ritual like individual confession.

> Some years ago a young woman came to me tortured with the guilt born with her illegitimate child, compounded by the cankerous secret kept even from the father of the child. I listened long. I spoke of what *I* knew of the forgiving grace of God. I wrapped both the time for speaking and the time for keeping silent in what *I* thought were the luminous, revealing veils of scripture, to no avail. Finally, moved by an unmistakable prompting, I took her to the chapel and knelt with her in prayer. Then I stood while she still knelt, placed my hand upon her head and said, "Rebecca" (this is, of course, not her name), "Rebecca, I forgive

you in the name of God. Now go, and live as a forgiven woman." I could tell you of the creative, restorative consequences in her life, but that is not my present point. My point is that we Protestants need some such pointed, specific, tangible counterpart to the Roman confessional.[16]

This example illustrates the important distinction that has to be made between the *preaching* of forgiveness and the *proclamation* of forgiveness. Psychology speaks of the negative "demonic" elements within ourselves—negative aspects of our characters which are further affected by wrong decisions, selfishness, and all the unconscious and half-conscious behavior that holds us back from discernment and fully free choice. The demonic within ourselves has to be objectified, brought to consciousness and laid out on the table if we are to deal with it and grow beyond it. Professional therapy helps us to do this. So does good preaching, and any competent analyst knows that there are religious dimensions to the demonic which therapy must take into account.

Good counseling and good preaching have this in common: they help us to objectify the demonic. They point out the need for healing, and each in its own way speaks of the things that enter into healing. Both the preacher of the gospel and the counselor tell us in different ways what we need to know about ourselves if we are to become human and whole.

The good counselor, the good therapist, the good preacher all have this in common: they are able to say "You are acceptable." But there is an essential thing beyond this, well exemplified by Garrison's story. All good counselors or therapists accept the person with whom they are dealing; but they are not able to speak for anyone but themselves. This is where "absolution," the sacramental proclamation of forgiveness, gets its force. This proclamation goes beyond the individual, beyond the personal relationship of therapist to patient, of counselor to penitent, of preacher to hearer of the word. It speaks of a community in which one is accepted, whatever one's past may have been. Good preaching and counseling says, "You are *acceptable* to the community." The laying on of hands, together with whatever words go with it, say, "You are *accepted* by this community."

All of this points to the abiding need for a "special" sacrament of reconciliation. But we still have to deal with the fact that the Catholic practice of confession has involved a kind of spiritual overkill. The special sign became a regular and ordinary sign, a monthly or even weekly part of Catholic religious practice, and this led to formalism and the deterioration of a profoundly meaningful ritual.

Many sincere Catholics feel indifference toward the confessional or positive distaste for it. Many are emotionally incapable of using confession for the purpose for which it was intended, because of their bad experience with it in the past.

This brings us to the question of communal celebrations and general absolution. What is the purpose of such celebrations? How do they differ from individual confession?

Contrary to the rules of good writing, let me begin

with the negative side. One hears stories of general absolution being used as a substitute for a real process of conversion. Or one hears of pastors using general absolution as a means of escaping the ministry of the confessional. One also gets the impression that the horror stories are the only stories the hierarchy hears. Hence the restrictions which at present surround the use of general absolution.

But there is real reason for caution. Absolution is not magic, and communal magic is no better than individual magic. As I suggested earlier, unless we overcome the superstition that has been associated with individual absolution, it is bound to carry over to general absolution.

Absolution is a sacramental action which rounds off a whole process of forgiveness and reconciliation. This implies that general absolution cannot suddenly be "laid on" a parish. It needs preparation, and it should be the *sacramental rounding-off of a whole communal process of renewal.* The directions of the new rite apply as much to general absolution as to individual confession: "Faithful Christians, as they experience and proclaim the mercy of God in their lives, celebrate with the priest the liturgy by which the Church continually renews itself" (#11). Unless it has been preceded by a communal experience of renewal, general absolution is liable to be a communal experience of legalistic magic.

The anomaly here is the rules which at present govern the use of general absolution. The rules were given considerable publicity during 1978, when certain Vatican officials and at least one American bishop disagreed, painfully, on interpretation of the new rite of penance. At the moment, general absolution seems to be permitted only as a last-minute solution to a pastoral need, namely, not enough confessors or enough time for individual confessions. One presumes that this regulation was meant to prevent an irresponsible use of general absolution.

In fact, as is so often the case with legalistic solutions to pastoral problems, the rule ends up accomplishing the exact opposite of what it set out to do. An effective use of general absolution calls for thorough catechesis and careful preparation of the whole community. *But the present rules governing the use of general absolution virtually forbid preparing a community for such a celebration!* That is why I have called those regulations an anomaly. They make general absolution a second-rate proclamation of God's forgiveness. And they hinder catechists and pastors from the work of explanation and preparation, which everyone knows is essential for any new liturgical practice.

Perhaps this is another case of the need for people to change before the rules can change. A basic problem here, I think, is not to isolate the single moment of absolution from the total context of *communal celebration* of forgiveness. The canonical regulations in the new rite make no reference to the *different needs* that are met by communal celebrations and by individual confession. We have talked at length about the ritual for individual confession. Now what is the purpose of a *communal* ritual of forgiveness?

Primitive cultures, in their rituals of purification,

used vivid actions like washing or burning, driving away or spitting out, covering up or burying. We moderns need to recapture some of this. Basic human gestures are the foundations of ritual, and our modern rituals are no exception. Rituals originate as actions, not words. Ritual actions, including everything from simple gestures to elaborate dances, appear on the scene long before prayers come along to articulate in a verbal way the meaning of the action. In our Christian rituals, the *words* we use are nothing more than a way of making explicit what the *action* is already saying. The eucharistic prayer says what the action of breaking the bread and sharing the cup means. The words at baptism or at the anointing of the sick say what the pouring of water or the anointing with oil means. The words at a wedding ceremony say what the joining of hands and the exchange of rings mean.

But how impoverished our penitential rituals are! They have been mostly a matter of reciting words and hearing words recited in return. They lack gesture, action, the basic components of ritual. Which is more important in Garrison's example quoted a few pages back: the minister's word of forgiveness, or his action of standing and laying hands on the penitent?

One of the most basic problems with individual confession has been its symbolic poverty. The laying on of hands is the original gesture of forgiveness and acceptance. The presence of a screen between minister and penitent made this impossible, but the physical gesture remained a theoretical part of the rite: the rubrics required the minister to raise his hand during the absolution. Where the screen does not interfere, it is clear that the original gesture of laying on hands is called for.

Which is more important in a community celebration of penance: the *words and prayers* of the participants, or the *actions and gestures* which speak reconciliation and God's forgiveness? Most communal penance services I have encountered are strong on words, frequently very beautiful words, but weak on ritual actions which would give a basis for the words in touch and feeling. There are many traditional Christian symbols which can be brought into play in a penance ritual. Passage from darkness into light. The baptismal font, and actions relating penance to the waters of baptism. And of course, the laying on of hands and the kiss of peace.

One of the forms in the new rite combines a communal celebration with the opportunity for individual confession. I would suggest that this type of ritual is a transition between the old and the new. The combination of a communal celebration with individual confession, all in a single rite, has helped many people to relocate the meaning of individual confession in its ecclesial context. This has been important.

But it is also important to undo the medieval idea that until one has verbalized a list of sins, one has not engaged in a genuinely sacramental action. The "combination" type of ceremony has the potential of throwing even more emphasis on the mechanical recitation of a list. The time available makes it impossible for minister and penitent to engage in the kind of spiritual therapy and mutual prayer which gives individual confession its particular value. A trained community knows how to handle this format, and how to avoid mechanical recitation. There is also weighty symbolic value in seeing a friend or neighbor walk up to a priest for individual confession during a communal penance ritual.

But the experience of many communities is that this is an interim form. I would predict that eventually we will keep the individual and the communal rituals separate. They are different ways of proclaiming forgiveness, because they meet different needs.

We have talked at length about individual confession, and the needs such a ritual can meet. But communal celebrations meet a different need. I would suggest that *communal* celebrations are meant to perform a singular service of *raising consciousness about the meaning of sin,* in a way that individual confession cannot.

Chapters 3 and 4 talked about the experience of sin at a less-than-adult level of consciousness. The adult Christian knows that sinfulness is much more than defilement, and that a loving God is not the cause of human misfortune. But then along come crisis situations where feeling takes over, where intelligence and rationality and all that our heads tell us are no answer, situations which call on resources we don't possess or haven't developed, situations which put us at wit's end. What happens then? Often enough we can see how mistaken or inadequate judgments of ours have produced the crisis we are undergoing.

But sometimes we take a further step, or rather a step backwards, and regress to a mentality we thought we had long since put aside: God must be punishing me for something, I must be suffering a punishment for some rule I broke. This situation is intolerable. It involves God in my feelings of guilt and in a subtle way makes God an excuse for my own inadequacy or lack of responsibility.

This example (and I do not think it is an uncommon experience) indicates the need we have for rituals which will help us to *interpret and deal with* personal guilt. The primary function of any Christian community is to be a group of people who accept others and who help others to accept themselves, no matter what they have done. The world in its best moments wants peace and reconciliation, and every sincere person in the world wants acceptance and pardon.

The Christian Church is called by God to be explicitly what the world implicitly wants: a community in which mutual acceptance and forgiveness are a reality. This reality is expressed in the living behavior of the community and in the actions of worship which foster Christian self-consciousness—first in baptism, then in the eucharist, the ordinary Christian ritual of acceptance.

But the Christian community also has a need to come together occasionally for special rituals of penance. As I see it, community celebrations of penance have at least three important functions, all of them authentically *sacramental* functions.

The first is to make explicit in the minds of the faithful what is implicit in any eucharistic celebration: that the Church exists for no other purpose than to be a community of reconciliation, a body of reconcilers. History shows clearly enough that this dimension of the eucharist fades all too easily. Preaching needs to renew and support it, including the especially forceful type of preaching involved in the gestures and actions of a special ritual of reconciliation.

A second function is that of working against our natural psychic tendency to suppress guilt and personal failure rather than deal with it consciously. This is the tendency of the unconscious to absorb sin and generate a kind of pseudo-forgiveness or self-justification. Individual confession has a singularly important role to play here. But the private ritual needs reinforcement from a community liturgy which emphasizes the communal and social dimension of human sinfulness. When the communal sense of sin is lost, personal and individual guilt becomes isolated, sin tends to become once again a "stain," and the psychic dynamic which wants always to drag us back to a more primitive religious consciousness goes to work in us.

This points to a third essential function performed by communal rituals of penance, namely, to provide a context in which personal guilt is joined with reflection on communal responsibility and thus kept from turning in on itself. Christian consciousness of sin either fades into vagueness (I am a sinner like everybody else—so what?) or turns into an intolerable burden (I *am* a sinner and *my* sins are unpardonable) when we lack sacramental rituals in which we can locate our personal experiences of failure and inadequacy, *deal* with personal sin at a conscious level and begin to overcome it.

A communal ritual should therefore help people to do what this book has so often discussed: to go beyond *sins* to an awareness of *sinfulness.* The formula sometimes used at the beginning of mass, "Let us call to mind our sins," is a most unfortunate expression; its intention is obviously good, but it invites the listener to reflect on much too little, and maybe on the wrong things. We need to overcome the separation between "religionized sins" and the real experiences of sinful*ness* which fall outside the categories of mortal and venial, nameable and numberable actions.

This is especially important for children who, preoccupied as they naturally are with learning the rules of the game of life, need religious rituals which will lead them beyond the experience of rule-breaking, which is basically the primitive experience of defilement. This suggests what contemporary psychology, theology and catechetics have been urging, and what many parents have prudently decided: that a child's first experience with sacramental penance should be communal celebrations of penance, not individual confession.

"Sins" are isolated acts which too easily become substances or stains. The real human problem, and the level at which the gospel calls us to operate, is to deal with the *motives and attitudes* which generate our actions.

We have talked about this distinction so often that it must be tiresome by now. The problem is that while good preaching tries to reach motives, penance rituals often remain a forum for dealing with little more than isolated acts and violations of set precepts. In fact, it should be one of the key functions of a penitential ritual to raise consciousness above the level of observance of the commandments.

What we know as the "ten commandments" are drawn from an ancient Hebrew code which does not in fact involve any special revelation of Yahweh to his chosen people. Equivalent precepts are found in Mesopotamia and elsewhere in the ancient world. Western culture has adopted the decalogue (at least in theory) not just because of its ratification by Judaism and Christianity, but because the decalogue contains fundamental human wisdom. It suggests moral principles that are essential for the survival of any society.

But at the time the commandments were formulated, no one would have conceived of a young child's disobedience as an offense against the commandment to "honor your father and mother," or of a minor lie or dishonesty between otherwise good friends as an act of "bearing false witness against your neighbor." We have used the ancient commandments as a framework for interpreting values and moral preoccupations which do not at all belong to the original understanding of these commandments.

There is nothing intrinsically wrong with this. We do the same thing when we apply principles of the eighteenth-century American Constitution or Bill of Rights to twentieth-century situations. Of course, adaptation of the biblical commandments to contemporary situations becomes tenuous in the examples I gave in the last paragraph. It becomes downright ridiculous in other applications which one can find in all too recent catechisms—as when masturbation (wasting semen) is an offense against the commandment not to kill, or when feeling aroused is the moral equivalent of adultery or coveting another's wife.

My point is simply that the ten commandments are not sacred and do not constitute an essential focus of Christian education. The commandments have been reinterpreted throughout western history, expanded to include all sorts of minutiae, and also contracted to *exclude* many kinds of real sinfulness. People today, for instance, are being forced to face all the qualifications and just-war theories which centuries have laid onto interpretation of the commandment "You shall not kill." The framers of that commandment would be shocked to discover how much killing we allow, all the while giving assent to the fifth commandment!

Today's catechetical techniques have de-emphasized the commandments, and this disturbs a good many parents. Perhaps adults who worry over the absence of emphasis on the commandments need first to question the Christian values—or lack of values—which they have themselves associated with the traditional commandments. What is the function of the commandments as a catechetical device?

Obviously anyone brought up in our culture will learn the Decalogue and the basic moral principles it implies. But I repeat the question: What is the function of the commandments as a *catechetical* device? Do the traditional commandments *raise* Christian consciousness, or do they simply affirm what every sensible and sensitive human being already knows?

This is not really a new question. Matthew was dealing with basically the same idea when he depicted Jesus as the new Moses, presenting a new law. In the "fulfillment" motif of Matthew's gospel, the beatitudes of the sermon on the mount replace and supersede the commandments given to Moses on Sinai. I mentioned earlier that one of the essential functions of a penance ritual is to provide a context in which personal guilt is joined with reflection on communal responsibility.

There are many ways to work this out ritually. One way might be to follow Matthew's lead and reflect on a standard of behavior that goes beyond the commandments. In the following confession, the leader pauses after each set of petitions to allow time for private reflection.

Leader: Blessed are you, Father, for giving the kingdom of heaven to the poor in spirit.

All: Forgive us for the times we have put our own comfort above all else, and for using selfishly the good things you have given us. Pardon us for our failure to realize we are spiritually poor and need your help at all times, even when we succeed.

Leader: Blessed are you, Father, for giving the earth as a heritage to the gentle.

All: Forgive us for our arrogance and self-centeredness in going after the good things of the earth. Forgive us for abusing the earth and exhausting it.

THE FORGIVENESS OF SIN

Forgive us for the way we have trampled on the earth and on other people, to get what we want and to have our own way.

Leader: Blessed are you, Father, for comforting those who mourn.

All: Forgive us for the times we have failed to bring comfort to people who have come to us in need or in suffering. Pardon us for being so self-centered that we could not even recognize people in need.

Leader: Blessed are you, Father, for satisfying those who hunger and thirst for what is right.

All: Forgive us for our attitude of seeking our own will, right or wrong. Forgive us for hungering and thirsting after things without even thinking about whether they will help us to serve you.

Leader: Blessed are you, Father, for showing mercy to the merciful.

All: Forgive us for failing to forgive others. Pardon us for passing judgment on others, and for the enjoyment we have taken in criticizing others.

Leader: Blessed are you, Father, for showing yourself to the pure of heart.

All: Forgive us for the times we have thought of others or used others for the sake of our own pleasure. Pardon us for our unwillingness to accept our sexuality, for running away from it rather than seeing and using it as a gift from your hands.

Leader: Blessed are you, Father, for giving the name of children of God to peacemakers.

All: Forgive us for the times we have made war on others in our hearts. Forgive us for brooding over hurts and grievances. Pardon us for the times we have come to your altar without first reconciling ourselves with our brothers and sisters.

Leader: Blessed are you, Father, for giving the kingdom of heaven to those who are persecuted in the cause of right.

All: Forgive us for failing to accept suffering in our own lives, and for bringing suffering to others. Forgive us for persecuting, in our hearts and in our actions, those who do not see things our way. Pardon us for hesitating to hear your word and doing it, out of fear of being persecuted as Jesus was.

A communal confession of this sort needs sights and sounds and actions, non-verbal signs to go along with the verbal confession: the kiss of peace, the laying on of hands, the lighting of a candle in the darkness, evocation of the water of baptism, the breaking of the bread. A film or some other audio-visual device might frame the liturgical action and provide a stimulus for reflection. Scripture should be well chosen (sometimes there is too much of it, too many words).

As for the confession itself, I readily admit that a formula like the one I have given develops contemporary ethical implications from the beatitudes in just the same way as another age worked its moral preoccupations into the framework of the ten commandments. The problem is neither the formula of the Old Testament commandments nor the formula of the New Testament beatitudes, but rather the raising of moral consciousness to the level at which today's Christian should be dealing with sin and reconciliation.

In a famous page in the history of worship—the account of covenant renewal given in the Book of Joshua—the people are asked whether or not they want to go on with the covenant with Yahweh. Joshua told the people: "If it does not please you to serve the Lord, decide today whom you will serve, the gods your fathers served beyond the river or the gods of the Amorites in whose country you are dwelling. As for me and my household, we will serve the Lord" (Josh 24:15).

Our Christian rituals have often overlooked the principle implied in Joshua. We glibly speak of the freedom to decide, the freedom to say yes or no. Decide *what?* Say yes or no to *what?* Our ordinary worship too easily implies that we already know everything we are saying yes to. The fact is, we are never finished with the task of formulating just what *our* values are as a Christian community *today.* The planning of a community liturgy of penance along with the celebration of it can thus provide a unique opportunity for a contemporary "covenant renewal." This form of sacramental penance should help us to articulate what we try to become as a community of reconciliation, whenever we gather to proclaim to anyone who asks it: "In the name of God, you are accepted."

As we look at the different ways of celebrating reconciliation, it is important to keep in mind a key sentence from Vatican II: "It is to be stressed that whenever rites, according to their specific nature, make provision for communal celebration involving the presence and active participation of the faithful, this way of celebrating them is to be preferred, as far as possible, to a celebration that is individual and quasi-private."

If this statement from the *Constitution on the Sacred Liturgy* (#27) is taken seriously, it is clear that general absolution, properly understood, is not a second-rate proclamation of God's forgiveness. Quite the opposite. Once the moment of general absolution is placed within a context of community renewal, it is clear that *communal celebrations of penance take precedence over individual confession.*

But if this precedence in theory is ever to become a reality, we need to do much more reflection on the *different needs* met by the two different rites. They are two different forms of *celebration,* and they celebrate different experiences. This chapter has tried to sketch a few of the differences. Behind the differences lies the basic problem that has been such a consistent theme in this book: We have to move beyond the concept of absolution as legal pardon, and acquire a deeper sense of what we are doing when we dare to proclaim God's word of forgiveness.

Chapter 10

REPENTANCE: OLD WINE IN A NEW JUG?

We have tried, pastor and theologian, to cover all the bases laid out by the new rite of penance. There is no last word to be said, happily, because the experience of forgiveness and reconciliation is ever new. The experience is bigger than any theological categories, and it is always a newest and most magnificent thing to any pastor who is privileged to share in it.

So what shall we do in a final chapter?

We have decided to offer you a kind of examination of conscience—or better, a way of examining one's conscience in the light of the many things that have been said in the last nine chapters. This chapter will put together a bit of the old, some words from St. John Chrysostom, who died in the fifth century—and a bit of the new, which talks about our own present-day experience of repentance. All along the way, we'll be talking about the kind of experience to which the Church's new rite of penance invites us.

Embedded deeply in the American mentality is the conviction that there must be a winner and there must be a loser. There is no in-between. The news media reinforce that conviction. Take election night, for example. Computer analysis predicts that Joe Go will win over Lou Lews. Immediately the camera is switched to Joe Go's election headquarters. Pandemonium has broken loose. People are hugging and kissing one another, champagne is flowing, and Joe Go with his wife and children, looking much like the cat that cornered the mouse, is preparing to give the usual patronizing and condescending trivia known as the acceptance speech.

That ritual finished, the cameras swing us over to Lou Lews' gloom room where pain reigns. Beer may be near, but the room is champagne-less. With no hugs, no kisses, and with a few last hurrahs, loser Lou Lews, probably wondering how he'll pay for this mess, can think of nothing more brilliant to say than "We came in second but we tried harder."

This winning-and-losing syndrome, with absolutely nothing in-between, has made it difficult for American Catholics to understand the mentality of the new rite of penance. The new rite suggests that confession, repentance, and reconciliation are part of the process of growing in Christ. With our legalistic approach to sin, we go to confession as losers and we leave the church as winners. I broke a law. That makes me a loser. I'm "on the outs" with God because I'm a law breaker. I go to confession. I get straight with the law. I'm in with God again. I'm a winner.

We Americans are so task-oriented that we miss the beauty along the way. When I view TV scenes like

Lou Lews' "Paradise Lost," I wonder about the friendships that were made in the community that may have been formed as all those people worked together to get their man into office. Is happiness only in the conquest? Or is it also in the pursuit? Does a projected computer analysis on election night wipe out the beauty, the honor, and the glory of the pursuit? Is winning the all-embracing transcendent reality nullifying whatever growth, integrity, and wholeness may have been realized on the way? Wholeness is not a matter of winning and losing. It is a matter of growing. If this "in-between" reality is not reckoned with, both winners and losers are losers.

No one who celebrates the sacrament of penance is a loser unless that experience fails to raise his or her consciousness to the one truly transcendent and all-embracing reality—God really loves me! I lose only to the extent that I am unaware of his loving, saving, and intervening presence in every moment of my life. If I don't recognize that the Risen Christ is with me, is truly Emmanuel, along the way to eternity, I am to that extent a loser. If all I seek to win is favor with law, then I have already lost the tremendous beauty of Christianity.

It is this beauty the new rite offers to us. It calls for a conversion whereby we arrange our lives in such a way that they become responses to God's love. This arranging of our lives is a lifelong process. If there is any losing to be done, it is a dying to an old arrangement of life built around ego-centricity, erotic motivations, and trivial values. Jesus put it this way: "I am telling you not to worry about your life and what you are to eat, nor about your body and how you are to clothe it. For life means more than food, and the body more than clothing. . . . Set your hearts on his kingdom, and these other things will be given you as well" (Lk 12). That's what you call rearrangement.

Winning and losing with nothing in-between may have caused many people to give up on confession, or any other form of the sacrament of penance. A person who time after time leaves confession feeling that he has won, only to discover the next day that she has lost again, is bound to become disillusioned with the sacrament. The new rite says that there is an in-between process, that the battle against ego-centeredness is never-ending, that there is something that we can do about it, and above all that God loves us throughout the whole process of rearranging our lives. Take repentance for example. This is not an "I found it" ego-trip the pharisees were on. "I thank you, God, that I am not grasping, unjust, adulterous like the rest of mankind, and particularly that I am not like this tax collector here. I fast twice a week; I pay tithes on all I get" (Lk 18). Yes, he had made it. He had reached the pinnacle of holiness because he had kept the law! He was a "winner".

Nevertheless, the "loser" won the respect and love of Jesus. Yes, the publican had sinned. He was guilty of all the irregularities pharisees abhorred. But he was conscious of the one and only saving reality a legalistic arrangement of values blinded the pharisees to. He believed that God loved him and that around the love and mercy of God, not laws, he could rearrange his life. "This man, I tell you went home at rights with God; the other did not."

How do you go about this rearranging process? It begins with repentance, and while repentance is a gift of God, there are some paths we can take to repentance. St. John Chrysostom lists five paths of repentance.[17]

1. "A first path of repentance is the condemnation of your own sins: 'Be the first to admit your own sins and you will be justified.' For this reason, too, the prophet wrote: 'I said: I will accuse myself of my sins to the Lord, and you forgave the wickedness of my heart.' Therefore, you too should condemn your own sins; that will be enough reason for the Lord to forgive you, for a man who condemns his own sins is slower to commit them again. Rouse your conscience to accuse you within your own house, lest it become your accuser before the judgment seat of the Lord."

Admission of sin is on two levels. I can admit that I did certain sinful acts. I may be sorry that I acted the way I did. I may even condemn my behavior. But my admission, sorrow, and condemnation really pertain to something outside myself. I am repenting of acts which can't be changed because they are in the past. I may not, however, be repentant of something that can be changed. Here is where I need to move into the second level of admission or condemnation. I need to admit that my sinful acts flow from an interior, sinful, habitual attitude which forms and determines the ways I act. At this point I move in on myself. I move in on ego-centeredness, and that's where the real action is when it comes to repentance.

REPENTANCE: OLD WINE IN A NEW JUG?

To admit that I am wrong, that I am diseased, and that I am sinful, is a lot more painful and humiliating than to admit that past and irrevocable sinful actions were wrong, diseased, and painful.

The person who says, "I will never do these actions again," is not necessarily repentant and may do them again. But the person who says, "I condemn this de-rangement within myself and will make a change in myself," is on the path to repentance. "Rouse your conscience to accuse *you* within your own house" is Chrysostom's way of saying that repentance does not lie in my sinful actions, but in the recognition that I am sinful.

This first path to repentance is at the heart of the problem with people who say, "I confess the same old sins again and again," or who say, "I don't know what's sinful anymore." Merely confessing or reciting sinful actions will never lead to healing and to sinlessness. But admitting, painful as it is, that I am a sinful person and have let my sinfulness twist and warp my person and personality is the beginning of repentance.

Admission of sinfulness on this second level is truly a path to God. This is the level and the path where the publican found himself. It is also where Jesus Christ found him. Here is where real cleansing takes place. God moves into our lives with lightning speed when we find the honesty, the openness, and the courage to say, "God be merciful to me a sinner."

All of this makes me wonder if the spirit of the new rite isn't, after all, getting through to us. Perhaps the realization that the new rite is really calling for a complete rearrangement of our lives, lock stock and barrel, is at least partially responsible for empty pews and unused reconciliation rooms.

I don't believe that the revision of the sacraments has been a failure. The message has been loud and clear. A lot of people see the implications of that message and perhaps are no more ready to change their lives than those who followed Christ looking for cures and cuisine. Jesus offered much more than this in exchange for following him. He offered a new life completely arranged around him and his values. That journey takes a lifetime along the pathway of repentance. The new rite of penance clearly voices God's call to change our lives, to condemn our sinfulness, and to follow Jesus who leads to wholeness and holiness.

2. "Another and no less valuable path to repentance is to put out of our minds the harm done to us by our enemies, in order to master our anger, and to forgive our fellow servants for their sins against us."

During my senior year in high school, the highway patrol presented a movie on driving safety. One interesting fact sticks in my memory and has influenced my own driving habits. I learned that all of us with normal eyesight can count on two kinds of vision, focused vision and peripheral vision. For example, I can focus directly on one object in a room, and at the same time, with peripheral vision, see many other objects in the room. Peripheral vision not only enables us to keep our balance, it is often a real lifesaver. With peripheral vision we can be alerted to all kinds of danger not in our direct line of focus.

Fast driving, however, narrows down our peripheral vision and reduces it to direct focus on the highway. The fast driver sees nothing but the highway before him, and to that extent is blinded to the many potential dangers normally seen in peripheral vision at slower speeds.

In just the same way, people who focus entirely on real or imagined hurts inflicted by another lose all sense of balance and perspective. All of life becomes what their hurt is. Their family, friends, business associates, or fellow workers, move out into the periphery of life, eventually to be lost sight of as they race through life bent on getting revenge. As time goes on they rearrange everyone and everything around their hurt pride. If they can get away with it they will involve the members of their family, friends and associates, in their avenging intent. If they have retained any semblance of religion, they imagine God to be on their side as they enter into a conspiratorial relationship with him.

Such people are on the path of self destruction. They are incapable of listening to reason because their hurt roars in their ears. They are incapable of seeing dangerous developments surfacing in their family, work, mental outlook and spiritual orientation.

Nursing hurts is an addiction as real and as harmful as alcohol and drugs. Just as a person arranges all of life around the bottle or needle, so the brooder of hurt ego arranges his or her life around wounded pride.

"Putting out of our minds the harm done by our

enemies" is a daily exercise of the virtue of penance. Ignoring slights, putdowns, snubs, and a variety of tasteless barbs by equally tasteless and boorish people is penance far more rigorous than perhaps the more observable and staged rigors of abstinence from food, beverages, and cigarettes. As a matter of fact, I have often wondered if such abstinence is not a cop-out for the more rigorous yet healing abstinence from the self-indulgent and self-pitying exercise of brooding over hurt feelings. I do not oppose external penances as long as they express an on-going interior renewal. What benefit is there when in the name of piety, I re-arrange my eating and drinking habits but all the while continue to let my interior life be arranged around the self-pity of an inflated ego?

I'm astonished at the number of people who condemn the "softness" of today's Church and who want to go back to the "toughness" of yesterday's Church. If I thought that external fasting by itself would lead me to repentance and holiness of life, I'd be the first to get tough about the old ways. But Isaiah makes me quite nervous about this: "What are your endless sacrifices to me?" (Isaiah 1: 11). I think true repentance begins with much tougher stuff.

3. "Do you want to know of a third path to repentance? It consists of prayer that is fervent, careful, and comes from the heart."

When I was nine years old, I decided to be a pianist. I suppose I wanted to play the piano for the same reason the mountain climber decided to climb Mount Everest—"It was there."

In those 1930's depression days piano lessons were

a luxury for the family. That didn't stop me. I learned to play it anyway. From that time until I went to college I practiced the piano about four hours a day. After that I slackened off to two hours a day. Even now, at age 56, I manage to get in a little tickling of the ivories every day.

I wish I had a dollar for every time I heard people say, "I'd give anything to play the piano like that." Whenever I hear that said, I usually smile sweetly and go on playing the piano. There is no point in responding because chances are the person would not in fact "give anything to play like that." What the statement really means is, "I'd like to play the piano if there were a magic wand to make me play like that —now!"

There are no magic wands for expertise in anything, including prayer. It is interesting that the Latin word for work, *laborare,* also contains the Latin word for prayer, *orare.* St. Benedict's motto, *ora at labora,* is right on target. It is also interesting that when St. Ignatius schooled his followers and students in the art of praying, he called his method "spiritual exercises."

Prayer is work. Prayer that is fervent, careful, and from the heart is impossible to the sporadic pray-er. The way many of us pray reminds me of the story of the Sunday-school teacher who wrote on the blackboard, "God is like—," and asked her class of 4th graders to fill in the blank. A little boy wrote: "God is like Alka Seltzer, good to have around when you get upset." Well, if God is nothing more than a heavenly Alka-Seltzer tablet, you can bet prayer will be a fizzle.

Prayer is not what we do to God. Prayer is what God is endeavoring to do in us. Prayer is not our trying to get God's attention; prayer is God trying to get our attention. What we think we need is very far from what God knows we need. Prayer that is fervent, careful, and from the heart makes us aware of God's loving presence and also our poor response to that presence. Prayer is God's light showing us the riches we already have. Prayer is not for upset people only; prayer is for people who are ready to sit up and take notice of the God who is already so fully in their midst.

We don't pray to find God. We pray so that God can find us and bring us back to the path of repentance. Poet Francis Thompson described God as the hound of heaven whom he had fled "down the nights and down the days, down the arches of the years, down the labyrinthine ways." This, I believe, is the choicest fruit of prayer when, poor in spirit from fruitless and mindless meanderings, we discover that all the while God has really been pursuing us: "Ah, fondest, blindest, weakest, I am he whom thou seekest!"

Here's where repentance begins and "prayer that is fervent, careful, and from the heart" can lead us to that path.

4. "If you want to hear of a fourth path to repentance, I will mention almsgiving, whose power is great and far-reaching."

What emerges in St. John Chrysostom's five paths

of repentance is the Church's own ageless program for repentance, prayer, fasting, and almsgiving. Prayer creates a hunger for God. Fr. Edward Farrell has written a book entitled *Prayer is a Hunger.* Reading this book made me see how much time we waste praying to *get* things. Genuine prayer helps us see how much we already have, and enables God's spirit to groan within us for what we don't have, a craving for repentance, justice, and holiness.

Fasting is a necessary companion to prayer, and like prayer, presents us with another gift, a craving to exceed the mediocrity of human respect in order to attain integrity. Self-indulgence, whatever form that takes, is the real enemy of human development. And fasting exposes the extent to which we have allowed personal integrity to be sacrificed for the lesser appetites for self-gratification.

If prayer creates a hunger to see God, fasting surely creates a hunger to see ourselves as we really are. Both are remedies for the blindness which prevent us from seeing the injustice we inflict upon ourselves and upon the poor. Once that blindness is removed, repentance begins.

Almsgiving is a third hunger. A sure sign that God's holy spirit is at work within us is the generosity called almsgiving we find ourselves craving to do. Someone has said, "Almsgiving is post-operative care following surgery on selfishness."

Almsgiving is not the same as tithing. Tithing is due out of justice, almsgiving springs out of love. Tithing is rendered out of accountability while almsgiving is rendered out of responsibility. Tithing is a debt due, almsgiving is a depth of God's love renewed. When one gives 10 percent of his earnings, he still retains the other 90 percent for himself. Almsgiving gets into that 90 percent. The widow's mite was not a tithe because she gave all she had. Her alms made the Pharisees' 10 percent look rather mite-y.

When Zacchaeus wanted to see what kind of man Jesus was like, he was in prayer. When he climbed the sycamore tree, forgetting the conventionality of his human respect, he was fasting. When he promised to repay those whom he had cheated fourfold (payment with interest) he was tithing. When he promised to give half of his property to the poor, he was almsgiving.

When Jesus said, "Blessed are they who hunger and thirst for holiness," he was not blessing hunger and thirst. He deplored the gross injustice of those whose greed fostered hunger and thirst. What he blessed was the all-consuming and desperate search for justice and holiness. He blessed those whose hunger and thirst for holiness and justice is as all-consuming as the search of the poor for food and drink.

I don't think anyone can generate hunger and thirst for holiness and justice by themselves. These are gifts of God's spirit. What we can do, however, is create the climate enabling God's spirit to activate an insatiable appetite for holiness and justice. That's why I see a lot of sense in the Church's simple formula for repentance—prayer, fasting, and almsgiving.

5. "If a person lives a modest, humble life, that, no

less than the other things I have mentioned, takes sin away."

While I was living in residence at the parish where I am now pastor, the church was constructed. The ground-breaking took place early in the summer of 1959, and the first Mass was celebrated in June 1960. What struck me most about the construction was the amount of time spent below the ground. Months went by before a single brick was laid above the ground. When the bricklayers began working, it seemed no time at all before the super-structure was completed. One visit to the foundation area of the building soon convinced me of the necessity of taking time below the ground. I saw electricians patiently sorting and connecting hundreds of wires. Just one bad connection would later on necessitate a search comparable to finding a needle in a haystack. Plumbers too were taking their time. Like the electricians, they did not relish a return visit to darkened tunnels in search of faulty plumbing.

During those years of greatly expanded building activity in our diocese, one of our pastors, Fr. Frank Osdeik, was a member of the Diocesan Building Commission. He was a terror. Many a blueprint went back to the drawing boards on his recommendation because the "footin's aren't right." He used to say, "Get the footin's right and the rest of the building will take care of itself." I am sure Fr. Osdeik is the reason a lot of time was spent below the ground in the construction of our parish church. As it turned out, I'm glad.

Humility is the "footin's" of our spiritual lives. It

is from the latin *humis* which means dirt. Just as foundations are laid in dirt, so the foundation of holy living is laid in humility. Upon this foundation of humility is laid the cornerstone, Jesus Christ, upon whom we the building rest.

St. Peter regarded Jesus as the cornerstone laid upon the foundation (1 Peter 2). Jesus, however, saw his words as the rock upon which the foundation is laid: "Everyone who comes to me and listens to my words and acts on them—I will show you what he is like. He is like the man who when he built his house dug, and dug deep, and laid the foundation on rock; when the river was in flood it bore down on that house but could not shake it, it was so well built" (Luke 6: 47–49). Jesus is both foundation for the foundation and cornerstone for the edifice.

Neither Jesus nor Peter used the word "humility" in the above quotations. And yet both contain the heart of what humility means. A humble person has no hidden agenda ("I have made up my mind, don't confuse me with the facts.") Such a person is ready to follow the advice of Peter: "Free your minds, then, of encumbrances: control them, and put your trust in nothing but the grace that will be given to you when Jesus Christ is revealed" (1 Pt 1, 13). It's the hidden agenda, the encumbrances, which prevent God's word from becoming the strength and the character of the super-structures of our lives.

Someone has written that Christianity hasn't failed, it hasn't even been tried. Humble people are ready to try Christianity because they are ready to let go of, or perhaps lose, the encumbrances, the hidden agenda, and the vested interests which prevent repentance and conversion.

Recently, I saw a bumper sticker which read, "God, guns, and guts made America great." In other words, God is okay and nice to have aboard, but just in case God doesn't "cut the mustard," guns and guts will. I wonder what's worse, out-and-out atheism, or a kind of polytheism which ranks God with guns and guts.

Humility is the readiness to let go of idols to try God and him alone. Polytheists really don't need humility because their guns and guts will always be handy just in case God doesn't fill the bill. When "God, guns, and guts," and "America, love it or leave it" is the new fundamentalism, why bother with the old gospel, "Come to me, listen to my words, and act on them"?

Saints are people who have let go of idols and have tried God. They discover what "poor in spirit" means. The poor in spirit are the people who let go of riches and strengths which polytheists idolize. The poor in spirit are happy because they understand what St. Paul means: "There is only Christ. He is everything. He is in everything" (Colossians 3: 11). Humility is the openness and the courage to make that discovery. Humility makes us "sure of the footin's." The decision to build the super-structure is easy after that, because those who are humble know God goes all the way "when the footin's are right."

NOTES

1. Abraham Maslow, *Religions, Values, and Peak Experiences* (Viking Press, 1970), pp. 30–31.

2. *Poems of Gerard Manley Hopkins* (3rd ed.; Oxford University Press, 1948), p. 70.

3. See Raymond Brown's discussion of this text in *The Gospel according to John,* Anchor Bible, vol. 29a (Doubleday, 1970), pp. 1039–1045.

4. *Didache* 4.14; cf. *Epistle of Barnabas* 19.12.

5. There have been countless articles and books on the history of penance in recent decades. I would recommend especially B. Poschmann, *Penance and the Anointing of the Sick* (Herder, 1964); and the fine collection of articles in *Sacramental Reconciliation,* ed. Schillebeeckx, vol. 61 of *Concilium* (Herder, 1971). For a good bibliographical survey, see *ibid.,* pp. 120–132.

6. Origen, *In Levit.* 2.4; cf. Poschmann, *op. cit.,* pp. 69–70.

7. Leo the Great, *Serm.* 88.3–4.

8. *Constitution on the Sacred Liturgy,* 10.

9. W. Kasper, "Confession outside the Confessional," in *The Sacraments: An Ecumenical Dilemma,* vol. 24 of *Concilium* (Paulist, 1966), p. 37.

10. From a sermon of 1519, quoted by David Belgum, *Guilt: Where Religion and Psychology Meet* (Augsburg Press, 1970), pp. 74–75.

11. From Luther's *Small Catechism,* 1529; quoted from Belgum, *op. cit.,* p. 76.

12. See Harry McSorley, "Luther and Trent on the Faith Needed for the Sacrament of Penance," in *Sacramental Reconciliation,* pp. 89–98.

13. *Decree on Penance* (1551), canon 9 (DS 1709).

14. William Barclay, *The Daily Study Bible: Acts* (St. Andrew Press, 1974), p. 68.

15. J.-M. Tillard, "The Bread and the Cup of Reconciliation," in *Sacramental Reconciliation,* p. 54.

16. E. J. Fiedler and R. B. Garrison, *The Sacraments: An Experiment in Ecumenical Honesty* (Abingdon Press and Fides Publishers, 1969), p. 93.

17. Hom. *De diabolo tentatore* 2, 6.